CW00394220

LANGUAGE AND TRAVEL GUIDE TO
CROATIA

LANGUAGE AND TRAVEL GUIDE TO
CROATIA

Robert Niebuhr
and
Bernd Scherak

HIPPOCRENE BOOKS, INC.
New York

Copyright © 2009 Robert Niebuhr and Bernd Scherak

All rights reserved.

For information, address:
  Hippocrene Books, Inc.
  171 Madison Avenue
  New York, NY 10016
  www.hippocrenebooks.com

Library of Congress Cataloging-in-Publication Data

  Niebuhr, Robert.
    Language and travel guide to Croatia / Robert Niebuhr and Bernd Scherak.
      p. cm.
    Includes bibliographical references.
    ISBN-13: 978-0-7818-1223-8 (pbk. : alk. paper)
    ISBN-10: 0-7818-1223-2 (pbk. : alk. paper)
      1. Croatia—Guidebooks. 2. Zagreb (Croatia)—Guidebooks.
    3. Croatian language—Conversation and phrase books—English.
    I. Scherak, Bernd. II. Title.

  DR1509.N54 2009
  914.97204'3—dc22   2008050173

Printed in the United States of America.

Contents

ACKNOWLEDGMENTS

First and foremost, we both would like to thank our respective governments for placing faith in each of us by financing academic studies in Croatia. Niebuhr is deeply grateful to the Fulbright commission for awarding him funding to study in Zagreb, while Scherak thanks his Austrian and Croatian sponsors for financing his studies at Zagreb's Faculty of Philosophy and Faculty of Law. The time that we spent in Croatia was very rewarding, and the friendships and experiences have remained with us. The support of our friends and family also proved vital to our success. The following list of these people is surely not all inclusive, but we do wish to single out Richard and Kathy Niebuhr, Ligia Gómez Franco, Sabine Geiger, Manfred Hartl, Paul O'Grady, Mathew Longo, Vjeran Pavlaković, Stephen Batalden, Danko Šipka, Thomas Butler, and Ramiro Oliva.

How to Use This Book

Congratulations for wanting to make Croatia your next vacation spot, and for choosing this book to help guide you in planning the perfect getaway. So, what makes the *Language and Travel Guide to Croatia* different from other travel books?

Language and Travel Guide to Croatia is a combination of travel guide, gastronomical handbook, and basic language tutor. This book goes beyond other travel aids because it not only gives you the details on where to go and what to see, but it also strives to help you, the tourist, with the most important and frequent things that you will do on your trip to Croatia—that is, eat and drink. Food is an important aspect of culture, and what better way to enjoy culture than to understand the dynamic and tasty side of what a country has to offer?

This book is organized to provide you with all the tools and skills necessary for an enjoyable and trouble-free trip. Our goal is to provide you with the right knowledge to arrive at your Croatian destination knowing what to expect in the days ahead. The book outlines where to go and tells you about everyday things that we all take for granted at home, like finding Internet service and how to use phone booths to make local and international calls. Our language section includes enough to clue you in on what is going on through some basic communication examples and a small grammar section; our hope is that these will provide you with the tools and the desire to delve deeper into Croatian culture and language and to keep coming back to Europe's hottest tourist destination. We then provide an in-depth look at the food and drink that you will encounter in Croatia. Starting off with a guide to restaurants and other eateries that you will be frequenting on your trip, the section continues with an overview of the different eating and drinking options; from salads to desserts, you won't be disappointed!

Our goal for this travel guide is neither to overwhelm you nor to take all of the adventure out of your vacation. Instead, the information serves as a guideline, or rather, a crash course on Croatia's geography, culture, people, history, food, and language. No matter if Croatia is your ultimate destination or if you are just passing through on a more extensive European trip, this guide to Croatia is your first stop!

Finally, you will find here only a few recommendations for specific restaurants or accommodations because of the rapid changes occurring in Croatia, and so that you, the traveler, can experience what you want and not what we want! To help you have a great vacation, we offer extensive information (especially Web sites) along with tips and tricks to aid in your decision-making process. Of course, we cannot be responsible for the information provided by the Web sites cited or for their continued presence online.

CROATIA OR THE BAHAMAS?

Not yet sure if your next holiday destination will be Croatia? You would be missing out on what millions of visitors to Croatia over the last fifty years have enjoyed. Flip through the following pages; take a look at a map or satellite images from programs such as Google Earth to see the beautiful islands, mountains, and Zagreb from a bird's eye view; and check out Croatia online. You'll be convinced that Croatia is the place for you!

Zlatni rat beach

The answer to whether Croatia has more to offer than "just" the beautiful coast, the thousands of islands, the good food, the unforgettable romantic evenings in the restaurants along the Riviera, and the sports possibilities is: "*Sto posto!*"—"100 percent." There are the world famous Plitvička jezera (Plitvice Lakes), historical cities such as Vukovar, Osijek, and, of course, the capital city of Zagreb! Although many great flight connections are opening up every day to various Croatian cities, most air traffic still comes through Zagreb. In addition, if you choose not to fly and instead tour Europe by car or train, you will certainly have the chance to check out Zagreb before heading anywhere else. When friends ask how much time they need to get to know the Croatian capital, given the many sides of this up-and-coming city, the varied possibilities for dining out, the people you are going to meet, the museums, festivals, cafés, mountains, clubs, the Sava River, souvenirs, and, last but not least, the sights—the answer is simple: Just enjoy!

PART I

General Information

CHAPTER 1

CROATIA AT A GLANCE

Croatia is one of the new countries that emerged out of the former Socialist Federal Republic of Yugoslavia (SFRY) when that country dissolved in 1991. Within the former Yugoslavia, Croatia already existed as a republic—similar to a state in the United States—with the capital city Zagreb as a major metropolitan center. The approximately 4.5 million inhabitants are predominately ethnic Croats who practice Roman Catholicism. Croats are proud of their independent state, and with good reason. Since the conclusion of hostilities in the former Yugoslavia, Croatia's economy has been strong, fueled by the tremendous growth in tourism. Tourism has been a major industry in Croatia since the 1960s, and although today it represents a sizeable

St. Stephen's Cathedral and Zagreb

share of the national economy, this is still not mass tourism. No mega theme parks or franchise hotels/restaurants dominate the scene. Instead, the Croatian tourist industry operates as one of the largest in Europe while focusing on the beauty of nature. Aside from the fascinating coastlines and sun-baked beaches, Croatia offers a wide range of cultural heritage in major cities like Zagreb, Split, and Dubrovnik. In addition to working on your tan or seeing the latest collection at an art gallery, you can taste wine in a vineyard or follow Janica Kostelić's Olympic-medal dreams on Croatia's ski slopes.

Timing Is Everything

It may be tempting to visit Croatia and tour the whole country at once; especially spending ample time on the coast. If your schedule does not allow you more than a week, try to choose what you would most like to visit, and focus on that. Croatia is a small country, but the many breathtaking locations will humble any traveler.

In case you are convinced that a seven-day trip should cover all the major attractions, the authors suggest the following tour as a way to see the very best that Croatia has to offer in such a limited amount of time. Although it may be better to look online to book such a tour well in advance (look for "Croatia tours" or "Croatia Cruises" online or contact your favorite travel agent at home), it is possible to plan the tour by yourself and leave out a few destinations if you decide to spend one more day in, say, Dubrovnik than planned:

Zagreb – Karlovac – Plitvice – Split – Dubrovnik – Zadar –
the islands of Pag, Rab, and Krk – Rijeka – Zagreb

While a trip by bus may be exhausting on hot summer days, a car offers you all the advantages of independence: You may stop anywhere and set your own schedule. In addition, if you have a tent and camping gear, you will always find a spot for the night without difficulties.

In case you prefer a backpacking trip through Croatia, an island-hopping tour using the public ferry and boat connection is probably the most attractive way to get a feeling for the Adriatic and a nice opportunity to get in contact with both locals and other tourists. To plan such a tour, look up bus connections from your place of arrival (probably Zagreb) to Dubrovnik. Then start to cruise north along the coast until you reach Rijeka. Take a look at Chapter 4 to find information on the most important connections.

FACTS AND FIGURES

Croatian Political Map (COURTESY OF THE UNIVERSITY OF TEXAS LIBRARIES, THE UNIVERSITY OF TEXAS AT AUSTIN)

Land Area: Total: 21,830 square miles. (Slightly smaller than the state of West Virginia.)

Climate: www.wordtravels.com/Travelguide/Countries/Croatia/Climate/. High-tourist season intersects with warm weather (May–September), when temperatures can range from 60 to 100 degrees Fahrenheit.

Neighboring countries: Bosnia-Herzegovina, Hungary, Serbia, Montenegro, and Slovenia

Coastline: 3,625 miles (mainland 1,104 miles, islands 2,521 miles)

Population: 4,491,543 (estimated as of July 2008)

Age structure: 0–14 years: 16.2 percent (male 373,638/female 354,261)
15–64 years: 67 percent (male 1,497,958/female 1,515,314)
65 years and over: 16.8 percent (male 288,480/female 465,098) (2006 est.)

Ethnic groups: Croats 89.6 percent, Serbs 4.5 percent, others 5.9 percent (including Bosniaks, Hungarians, Slovenes, Czechs, and Roma).

Religions: Roman Catholic 87.8 percent, Orthodox Christian 4.4 percent, other Christian 0.4 percent, Muslim 1.3 percent, other and unspecified 0.9 percent, none 5.2 percent.

Languages: Croatian 96.1 percent, Serbian 1 percent, other and undesignated 2.9 percent (including Italian, Hungarian, Czech, Slovak, and German).

Widely spoken foreign languages include German, Italian, Spanish, and English, and while generalizations are problematic, younger people seem to have a higher tendency to speak English.

Holidays: January 1 – New Year's Day
January 6 – Epiphany
*Easter Sunday and Easter Monday
May 1 – Labor Day
*Corpus Christi
June 22 – Anti-Fascist Resistance Day (commemorating World War II)
June 25 – Statehood Day
August 5 – Victory Day and National Thanksgiving Day
August 15 – Assumption Day
October 8 – Independence Day
November 1 – All Saints Day
December 25–26 – Christmas

*These holidays fall on different dates each year.

Visa: American citizens do not need to obtain a visa prior to arriving in Croatia; they are given a "tourist visa" upon entry to the country. This is valid for thirty days and is provided free of charge. If you wish to spend more than thirty days in Croatia, you will need to apply for a visa beforehand. Either the Croatian embassy in Washington, DC, or one of the three consulates in Los Angeles, New York, or Chicago can assist with this procedure. Be aware that just prior to the summer months, the Croatian mission to the United States is busy and your request might take longer. For full, up-to-date information, please consult the Croatian embassy's Web site: www.croatiaemb.org.

Contact information:

Embassy in Washington, DC
2343 Massachusetts Avenue NW, Washington, DC 20008
Telephone: (202) 588-5899
Fax: (202) 588-8936

Consulate in Chicago
737 North Michigan Avenue, Suite 1030, Chicago, IL 60611
Telephone: (312) 482-9902
Fax: (312) 482-9987

Consulate in Los Angeles
11766 Wilshire Boulevard, Suite 1250, Los Angeles, CA 90025
Telephone: (310) 477-1009
Fax: (310) 477-1866

Consulate in New York
369 Lexington Avenue, New York, NY 10017
Telephone: (212) 599-3066
Fax: (212) 599-3106

The **United States Embassy in Croatia** is located near the main airport in Zagreb (Zagreb Pleso), but due to security issues its accessibility is limited and generally requires an appointment in advance. The contact information is:

2 Thomas Jefferson Street, 10010 Zagreb
Telephone: 661-2200 (outside of Zagreb dial 1 first)
Fax: 661-2373
www.usembassy.hr

Customs Regulations: Export and customs regulations can be found on www.carina.hr in English, German, French, Italian, Czech, and Hungarian. In general, limits exist regarding the amount of alcohol and cigarettes a traveler may have, although governments and airlines alike are changing the regulations every day.

Currency: Kuna (*koo-nah*), abbreviated HRK. Many money exchange offices are scattered throughout major cities with varying rates of exchange. They are all relatively competitive and are open late and on Saturdays. If you do not see a dedicated money exchange office, all banks and post offices will be able to turn your dollars, euros, or pounds into Kuna. It is illegal to change money with individuals on the street, but the rate in any case is likely to be poor and the practice risky.

Credit cards are increasingly being accepted in Croatia, but always be sure to check at the particular establishment where you want to use it. Also check with your credit card company to inquire about any fees associated with its use abroad. The typical charges range from two to three percent of the purchase price, after conversion into U.S. dollars. All ATM cards from American banks should work well in the bank machines located throughout Croatia. While a large number of ATMs can be found in Zagreb or Dubrovnik, ATMs are not always available in small towns or villages.

Tolls: A number of new highways have been constructed since the late 1990s, making travel to and within Croatia easier and faster. Several of these highways, however, are toll roads, and it is always best to have some currency. If you drive into Croatia you can change a few dollars at the border or pay with euros (although you are sure to get change in kuna). Gas stations and modern American-style rest stops are not uncommon along the major highways but, unlike in the United States, not all restrooms are provided free of charge. You might be asked to pay 2 or 3 kunas to use the restroom. www.hac.hr

Electricity: Standard European two-point plugs at 220V, 50Hz. If you bring your laptop it should work fine without a voltage converter—simply purchase an inexpensive plug converter. Check your AC adaptor, though, just to be sure. The same goes for mobile phone chargers. Most other electronic devices will need a voltage converter that should be purchased prior to leaving the United States because you will know what you are getting and it will be significantly cheaper.

Landmines: Contact the Croatian Mine Action Center for further information: www.hcr.hr.

COMMUNICATIONS

Telephone

Most Croats use mobile phones, but as opposed to the system in the United States, the majority of people still use phones that operate on prepaid cards similar to pay-as-you-go plans in the United States. That is good news for the traveler with a removable GSM card, because your phone can have a GSM chip for Croatia installed and you can then purchase airtime as you need. The two main phone companies are Vip and HT (T-Mobile), but several other companies are entering the market. You will see plenty of signs in the city centers for these companies in stores offering both the GSM chips and the airtime credit. The rates for airtime for local calls are generally inexpensive, but international calls are quite expensive from any mobile phone. Alternatively, several international phone companies are enhancing their service networks to span the Atlantic; so if you are unsure if your phone can be used without installing a new GSM card, check with your mobile phone carrier and also inquire if your provider rents out short-term, so-called world cell phones. If your phone has a GSM card, be sure to check with your mobile provider to see if the phone needs to be unlocked first to accept Croatian cards. In any case, you can be talking with friends and relatives in the United States or in Europe, telling them how great Croatia is!

For travelers who are not interested in using a mobile phone, rest assured that there are plenty of public pay phones; these are not, however, coin operated like many in the United States. Instead, you must visit a kiosk, mini-market, or a post office and purchase a "**telefonska karta za govornicu**" (*tele-phon-ska car-tah zah goh-vore-neat-sue*) and use that in the phone. The operation of the phones is clearly explained on the phone (in Croatian, but with clear pictures).

To dial out of Croatia, first press 011 followed by the number you wish to call. If you are calling Croatia from abroad, the country code is 385; the major city codes are as follows: Zagreb 1, Split 21, Zadar 23, Dubrovnik 20, Rijeka 51, and Pula 52.

> **Emergency Numbers in Croatia:** (from your mobile phone) **112**, (from any phone) Police **92**, Fire **93**, Medical **94**, Road help **987**
> **Yellow Pages in Croatia:** www.mti.hr

The Internet

The Internet is not new to Croatia; the government of Croatia has virtually all of its offices represented online. For the tourist, the most important Internet sites are those relevant to your trip. In this book, we have tried to provide a listing of such Internet sites. While the fluid nature of the World Wide Web makes any such listing problematic, the sites listed here should serve as a suitable foundation for any Internet search. We have tried to provide sites first of all in English, but otherwise the Croatian-language version is given. Here are some of the most useful sites for a good start to planning your Croatian adventure:

> www.balkanholidays.co.uk
> www.croatia.hr
> www.croatiaapartments.net
> www.croatianhistory.net/etf/mljet.html
> www.croatia-official.com
> www.croatiaparadise.com
> www.croatia-travel.org
> www.dalmacija.net
> www.find-croatia.com
> www.histrica.com
> www.inyourpocket.com (Zagreb, Zadar, Rijeka, Osijek)
> www.portal-croatia.com
> www.premium-tours.com
> www.sightseeing.komarna.co.uk/mljet.html
> www.timeout.com
> www.travel.hr
> www.uniline.hr

Radio, Television, and Newspapers

The international program produced by Croatian Radio called "The Voice of Croatia" is targeted at Croats abroad, but it is also a good source of information for tourists. Broadcasts are often in English and air twenty-four hours per day via satellite and online. Dive into this resource for Croatian culture, music, and news at www.hrt.hr/hr/glashrvatske.

In tourist areas you may also find newspapers and periodicals in English: the *International Herald Tribune* and *Newsweek*, and possibly a few others. To stay up-to-date with world news, find your favorite newspapers online or ask in your hotel if you can get CNN World or BBC News over satellite or cable television.

Other Croatian Radio and TV Stations on the Internet

If, after a search, you do not find an appropriate "livestream" Internet radio, use your favorite search engine to find "**program/radio uživo**" (*pro-gramm/ rah-deo oo-zhiv-o*), live program/radio. That should yield plenty of results. Also, be sure to check out the following:

Earbugs DOT radio: www.radio.earbugs.net

Hrvatski radio 1, 2, 3, Sljeme, Rijeka, Pula, Osijek, Split, HTV1: www.hrt.hr (HRT uživo)

Narodni radio: www.narodni.hr

Net radio 5+: www.radio5plus.hr

Obiteljski radio: www.obiteljski.hr

Otvoreni radio: www.otvoreni.hr

Radio 057: www.radio057.hr

Radio 101: www.radio101.hr

Radio Cibona: www.radio-cibona.hr

Radio DeeJay: www.radiodeejay.hr

Radio Kaj: www.radio-kaj.hr

Radio Koprivnica: www.radio-koprivnica.hr

Radio Marija: www.radiomarija.hr

Radio Martin: www.radio-martin.hr

Radio Mrežnica: www.radio-mreznica.hr

Radio Plavi 9: www.plaviradio.hr

Radio Student: http://RadioStudent.RedirectMe.net

Radio Valis Aurea: www.rva.hr

Zagrebački radio: www.zg-radio.hr

CHAPTER 2

INTRODUCTION TO CROATIA

MODERN HISTORY AND FUTURE STRUGGLES: A DESCRIPTION OF THE HISTORY FROM INDEPENDENCE UNTIL TODAY

Croatia's natural beauty and richness have attracted human settlements from the very beginning of time, and the territory that is now Croatia has served as both a vital crossroads for numerous European peoples and as a center for trade, culture, and conflict.

Prehistory to the Dawning of the Modern Age

It is widely believed that in the time before recorded history, nomadic tribes of hunters and gatherers roamed the area of modern-day Croatia. These prehistoric peoples established temporary accommodations in scattered enclaves across the country, including the mountainous border region between Croatia and Slovenia and along the coast. The various museums in Croatia offer a taste of this prehistoric human presence through various relics, and you can also visit the town of Krapina, near the Slovenian border (on the main road to Maribor/Graz from Zagreb), which has a complete complex dedicated to this earliest period of life in Croatia.

A bit later, in the few centuries prior to Christ, various tribes of Illyrians, Celts, and Greeks arrived in the region. The Illyrian settlement grew to become the most significant over time, and it penetrated into all parts of the country. The question of where the Illyrians came from is still hotly debated by scholars because the history of this people remains unclear—including the question of who their descendents are today. Not only did Napoleon Bonaparte carve his "Illyrian Provinces" out of much of Croatian territory and make it a part of France, but today some myths trace the ancestry of the Albanian people to the Illyrians of old.

East met West when the Illyrian settlements were conquered by the powerful Roman Empire in 168 BC. Traces of Roman influence clearly predated this time of conquest, as can be seen from some of the architecture, especially along the coastal regions and the Istrian Peninsula. If you travel to the city of Split today, you will be able to tour the palace of the Roman emperor Diocletian. The impact of broader Roman civilization, though, remains debatable, since Rome had a difficult time maintaining control of its Adriatic possessions throughout this period. This is also true of areas such as present-day Romania and Bulgaria, where Roman control rarely extended beyond a few-days march from the army barracks. This lack of profound influence is also partly due to the ultimate downfall of Rome and the resulting chaos. For the next several hundred years, various tribes of people from the East—Slavs included—would move in and wear down the Romans through war.

Until approximately the seventh century, Slavic peoples were relatively unknown to the region, but once migration began, Slavs overwhelmed the other tribes and came to dominate the entire Balkan Peninsula, including Croatia. Over the next 200-year period, the Croats organized into two groups: one group was centered on the fertile Pannonian Plain in the north, and the other along the rocky, coastal region of the south.

This period of Slavic migration and settlement also coincided with a sweeping move toward Christianization that emerged as the greatest lasting legacy of Rome's downfall. Hereafter, Croatia would be associated with Roman Catholicism and linked with the West. These first Christians naturally followed the conversion example of Croatia's ruling elite, with a more thorough wave of Christianization coming only in later decades. It was difficult to convert the masses, though, because the political organization of the area suffered from disunity. A united Croatian kingdom did not exist; instead a series of duchies spread out and competed for power. The most influential duchy at this time was controlled by the founder of the famous Trpimirović dynasty, Trpimir I (845–864). His state expanded from the beautiful coastal city of Zadar to the river Drava, which today lies at the border between Croatia and Hungary. Fifteen years after the end of Trpimir's rule, in 879, Pope John VIII became the first pope to recognize a Croatian duke—Duke Branimir.

For the next several generations though, Croatia still remained administered by several noble lords. But Tomislav (910–928), a member of the Trpimirović dynasty, united the duchies and became recognized as the first true king of Croatia. A bit more than a hundred years later, this Croatian kingdom reached its greatest point under King Petar Kresimir IV (1058–1074).

There are two sides to all peaks: the up side and the down side. Unfortunately for the Croats of that time, the next two hundred years saw a relative decline in Croatian power on the Balkan Peninsula. Neighboring powers—Serbia, Bosnia, Hungary, and Bulgaria—competed with the Croats and proved invincible. In 1102, weary from decades of conflict, the Croatian rulers recognized that without external support they would not endure. As a result, they accepted King Coloman of Hungary as the rightful ruler of Croatia, and this marriage of the two kingdoms of Croatia and Hungary lasted until the twentieth century, enduring innumerable political and ideological changes.

More Threats Emerge

Soon, another overwhelming force emerged from the south—from the mighty Ottoman Empire—as it made its northward drive into the heart of Europe. This Ottoman expansion placed the entire Balkan Peninsula in jeopardy. Finally, the last outside power to come to control part of Croatia was the Venetian Republic, thanks to a mighty navy and excellent trade networks throughout the Adriatic and Mediterranean. These three principal actors—the Hungarian kingdom, the Ottoman Empire, and Venice—would all remain the dominant forces in Croatia for the next several hundred years.

The major and decisive events of this period resulted from the onslaught of Europe by the Ottoman Turks and Europe's reactions to it. The beginning plays like a broken record; that is, the Ottomans almost always won, and when they did not win, they could bring in substantial reinforcements and win the next battle. The Balkan kingdoms rarely united, had fewer resources to draw from, and suffered from slow lines of communication. As a result, the Croats soon found themselves on the front line of what seemed an unstoppable military machine emanating from Constantinople.

The Ottomans won a series of major battles, including the Battle of Mohács in 1526, in present-day Hungary. This rout of the powerful Hungarian-led forces left the other Balkan kingdoms powerless to resist any further advances by the Ottomans, and over the next hundred years, the Ottomans slowly extended their control over the entire area. Bosnia, Serbia, and most of Croatia fell to the Ottomans. But the sultan's armies had their eyes on a bigger prize—Vienna.

At the Battle of Mohács, the Hungarian king Louis II (Lajos II) died, and the resulting power vacuum caused the most serious realignment in central and southeastern Europe after the Ottoman conquests. The famous Hapsburg family, then a moderately successful dynasty with primarily German holdings, recognized the opportunity unfolding in front of them. When calls for help came from the Hungarian nobility, Ferdinand I (1503–1564) of the House of Hapsburg responded by virtually taking over most of Hungary. What little remained outside of his control was run by a rival Hungarian nobleman who operated as a vassal to the Ottoman sultan.

Although Ferdinand gained impressive amounts of land in 1527, he was forced to defend his capital city of Vienna from besieging Ottoman forces. Ferdinand won, and by 1534 his forces were pushing back the Ottomans. With his throne and lands now secure, Ferdinand's attention was directed at slowly forcing the Ottomans to retreat from Europe. Thanks to its proximity to Austria, Croatia was one of the first to be liberated from the Turks, and the heated action there lasted only until the end of the 1590s.

Vojna Krajina

The **Vojna krajina**—or "Military Frontier" as it is known in English—grew into the primary line of defense of the Hapsburg lands against further Ottoman conquests. This border covered a large defensible region, stretching from the mountains near the Adriatic Sea up to the plains of Eastern Croatia. Thanks to almost a hundred years of prior conflict, this entire area was largely deserted; to fill the void, the Austrian authorities (since the Hapsburg lands became associated with Austria) encouraged settlement by various peoples from across the region. Vlachs, Serbs, Croats, and others came to this military frontier and lived as free men in return for occasional military service against the Ottomans. What this meant in practice was that these groups of settlers were left largely to their own devices, and while free from certain financial responsibilities, they were forced to plunder villages and towns inside the Ottoman Empire for survival. In response, the Ottomans erected a similar system of relying on their subjects to pillage the areas under Austrian control, thus creating a system of normalized cross-border banditry.

By the 1700s, much of Croatia remained safe from the series of Ottoman incursions, but the Croats themselves still participated in the fighting. Over the years, Austria utilized Croatian soldiers in many of its wars, and as a result, Croats saw action all across the continent. The most stunning series of wars, engulfing the entire continent of Europe and realigning the European order, came after Napoleon Bonaparte's success in Revolutionary France.

The Modern Era

While Croats had fought alongside Austria in each of the wars waged against Napoleon, war finally reached Croatian territory with Napoleon's victory over the Austrians in 1804 and resulted in his decision to annex some Austrian territory. Much of modern-day Croatia and Slovenia became incorporated into the Illyrian Provinces and became legally a part of France. French power never really manifested itself completely in the provinces, despite French rule persisting until 1813. Although some French soldiers were stationed in Croatia and important changes did occur under Napoleon, daily life continued much as before. The most significant inroads made by the French were in regard to the legal system and to cultural policy. The French authorities recognized what they called Slavonian (a cluster of Slovenian and Croatian dialects) as one of the official languages within the provinces and made initial attempts to more fully develop and standardize this language. When the Austrians finally regained the territory during the chaos of Napoleon's downfall beginning in 1813, they reversed many of the Napoleonic policies aside from those concerning cultural rights. While it was easy to abolish French as an official language of the provinces since few actually spoke it, other issues such as freedom for Jews and the recognition of a Slavonian language resisted rollback following the defeat of France. Napoleon's defeat, nevertheless, failed to guarantee peace and harmony in the region because together with an Austrian revival came a backlash from other groups under Austrian control—most forcefully from Hungarians and Croats—that proved irresistible. Post-Napoleonic concessions by the Austrians included the establishment of the so-called Dual Monarchy—the Austro-Hungarian Empire—which created an amazingly complex system of governance.

Because of Hungary's historic claim to the Croatian throne, the Hapsburgs had recognized Hungary's right to administer much of Croatian territory. In contrast, the Austrian half of the empire controlled much of the Dalmatian coast once the Venetian Republic disappeared in 1797 at the hands of Napoleon himself. The situation of contested authority within the empire wreaked havoc on internal relations and led to ongoing and interminable disputes and rivalries that continued into the twentieth century. By 1914, the situation demanded reforms within the monarchy, and one man seemed to offer promise for creating a more equitable distribution of power—Archduke Franz Ferdinand. But with his assassination in Sarajevo, World War I began and put any spirit of reform on hold.

Many had hoped that war would unite the various peoples of Austria-Hungary through a common struggle and naturally bring about improvement; instead, the outbreak of war exacerbated the situation and eventually led to total devastation. War destroyed Austria-Hungary, along with the German Empire, the Ottoman Empire, and the Russian Empire, but the situation that arose in 1919 was totally unexpected.

The total power vacuum that existed in 1918–1919 left the victorious Americans, British, and French with a host of problems. The realignment of Europe in the wake of the war led to the creation of many small states in place of the former empires. Croatia then entered a new era of history and became a part of the new Yugoslav state—first called the Kingdom of Serbs, Croats, and Slovenes.

Time would show the dangers inherent in Croatia's inclusion into this multinational state of Yugoslavia. Competing views of what a Yugoslav state should look like gave Yugoslavia few opportunities to prosper during the interwar period (1919–1939). The Croats' Hapsburg heritage inspired them to envision a loose confederation as the most desirable form of statehood, while the victorious and traditionally independent-minded Serbs thought that a tight federal system was best. Racked by internal tensions, by the end of this period the country was unable to properly function. When the Nazis finally invaded Yugoslavia on April 6, 1941, they found a country weakened by almost twenty years of internal strife. Not surprisingly, in less than a week

Hitler's armies had rolled over the Yugoslav forces and achieved complete victory. The face of wartime Yugoslavia grew increasingly ugly as Hitler manipulated the local elites for his own purposes and exacerbated hostilities among the inhabitants of Yugoslavia.

The notorious Ustaša state, run by Ante Pavelić, became a reality through Nazi support, and once in power, Pavelić proceeded on a campaign of brutality and genocide. Unfortunately, the actions of the wartime Croatian government handicapped Croatia's bargaining power during the initial years of the new Yugoslav state that emerged in 1945.

During World War II, a great deal of fighting in Yugoslavia involved Croats and took place in Croatia. One of the most famous of all Croats, Josip Broz Tito, emerged in the postwar state as the foremost contender for power (you can visit his birthplace and one of his mansions in the village of Kumrovec, near the Slovenian border). Still during the war, Pavelić and his Ustaša state alienated many Croats—let alone Serbs, Gypsies, and Jews—and helped Tito to grow more powerful and popular despite his own crimes against certain ethnic groups and political competitors in Yugoslavia. Tito's final victory came in 1945, when his Partisan army succeeded in liberating most of Yugoslavia, including Croatia, from both the Nazis and their allies.

The Yugoslav Era

When Tito won control of Yugoslavia, he created a federal state based on the ideological principles of communism. As a result, workers reigned supreme in Tito's state, and Croatia's relatively advanced industrial base finally seemed to provide the potential for prosperity. As a constituent republic, Croatia flourished in comparison to its Yugoslav neighbors, but prosperity did not guarantee cultural rights and happiness for Croats.

In Tito's Yugoslavia, the most decisive event for Croatia came about in 1971, during the so-called Croatian Spring. In that year, a series of cultural issues came to a head following the contentious publication four years prior of the "Declaration on the Name and Position of the Croatian Literary Language," which requested the affirmation of Croatian culture within the state's legal framework. Some of the Croatian intellectual elite protested against the apparent dominance of Serbian language throughout Yugoslavia. Tito eventually threatened to use armed force in Croatia to calm the situation and then followed up with a widespread purge of the leadership throughout Yugoslavia. The situation then remained calm until the late 1980s.

An Independent Croatian State—Again

In 1991, Croatia and Slovenia declared independence from Yugoslavia, thereby unleashing another four years of sustained conflict. The responsibility for war lay primarily with the Yugoslav political elites, who failed to effectively solve problems between competing interest groups—cultural, economic, ethnic, political, and religious. Both Croats and Serbs exacerbated the various disagreements and did little to alleviate the legitimate grievances of all concerned groups. Furthermore, when war reached neighboring Bosnia, it grew increasingly grim, and atrocities such as in Srebenica shocked the world into action. This particularly ugly turn occurred as each side sought to control ethnically homogenous territory—that is, an ethnically clean area. By 1995, with the help of the international community, the war came to an end and stability returned to the Balkans. Croatia has been able to fruitfully exploit its independence and to seek closer ties with Western Europe. The rather nationalistic agenda of Croatian president Dr. Franjo Tuđman during this period at first alienated the Western powers, but since his death, Croatia's leaders have turned toward embracing the new century as a new chance to enter Western associations such as NATO and the European Union (you can visit Tuđman's grave at Zagreb's Mirogoj Cemetery). As of 2008, Croatia seemed poised to soon enter the European Union and benefit from its still newfound independence.

Tourism in Croatia

The modern history of Croatia has been marked by its inclusion in what is referred to now as the former Yugoslavia. Since the 1960s, when the government under Josip Broz Tito opened up and developed the Adriatic seacoast, Croatia has been host to millions of tourists and has had a well-developed tourist industry. Before that time, the Adriatic coast, while beautiful, was an underdeveloped and backwards region because of the poor quality of the soil for farming and the problem of inland transportation. The region looked outward and, as a result, Croats have diasporas in the Americas and the South Pacific. In many parts of the United States, you are sure to find some people whose ancestors hail from Croatia. A cursory glance at Croats around the world reveals a high level of culture and learning as well as great artistic skills. Thanks to some of the rocky terrain along the coast, many Croats learned trades such as working with granite and sculpting as master craftsman in the Italian states. The country's location on the Adriatic Sea has naturally led Croats throughout history to become historically great seamen, master shipbuilders, and tireless traders in the Mediterranean.

In the 1990s, war briefly interrupted the tourist trade in Croatia, but since the end of hostilities in 1995, tourism has skyrocketed. Croatia has a lot to offer tourists both in major cities like Zagreb and along the beautiful Adriatic coastline. While tourism in the interior is beginning to make a name for itself, the coastline has the most to offer travelers. And although this area is less known to American and Canadian tourists, for at least the last ten years the Croatian coast has been hailed as a "second Riviera" for Europeans. During the summer, the combination of spectacular weather, untouched nature, and inexpensive prices makes the Croatian coast a tourist favorite.

Chapter 3

Pronunciation and Grammar

Part I: Pronunciation

Throughout the book, we have provided phonetics after every Croatian word to help you pronounce them correctly. Here we want to provide you with a more in-depth guide for your reference:

Croatian Letter	Croatian Example	Approximate Sound	English Example
A a	antena	*a*	father
B b	biftek	*b*	beef
C c	crven	*ts*	spots
Č č	čorba	*ch*	cheese
Ć ć	ćup	*tch*	gotcha
D d	dobro	*d*	dough
DŽ dž	džem	*j*	enjoy
Đ đ	đak	*dy*	jeep
E e	ekonomija	*e*	hen
F f	francuska	*f*	fish
G g	gladan	*g*	grab
H h	hrana	*h*	habit
I i	ići	*e*	ski
J j	jezik	*y*	Yugoslavia
K k	kifla	*k*	break
L l	led	*l*	love
LJ lj	ljubav	*ly*	magnolia
M m	majmun	*m*	mother
N n	nebo	*n*	no
NJ nj	njuška	*ny*	lasagne
O o	orada	*o*	orange

Croatian Letter	Croatian Example	Approximate Sound	English Example
P p	pljeskavica	*p*	opera
R r	riba	*r*	rinse
S s	sladoled	*s*	sever
Š š	šešir	*sh*	sure
T t	teletina	*t*	start
U u	ulje	*oo*	you
V v	v*lak*	*v*	vision
Z z	zelen	*z*	zebra
Ž ž	živjeli	*zh*	measure

PART II: GRAMMAR

Enjoying Croatian cuisine and traveling throughout the country does not require a mastery of the language. If you only frequent typical tourist areas, you will encounter waiters and others who know a bit of English if not German and Italian. Despite this, the more you know, the more pleasant your stay. That said, while it is not necessary to know all the rules of Croatian to be able to order in a restaurant, we have provided some basic grammar to help facilitate your use of some basic Croatian.

NOUNS

If you remember from elementary school, a sentence in English is constructed primarily of three parts—subject, verb, and object—often in that order. Croatian has the same components, but the grammar is more complex and the varieties of sentence construction more diverse. The next few pages are designed to give you a general understanding of some of the most common grammar you might use or encounter.

The subject of a sentence is in the nominative case, which is how the word is referenced in a dictionary. For example, **pivo** (*pee-voe*) "beer," or **jabuka** (*ya-booh-kah*) "apple." When ordering in a restaurant, for example, nouns must be indicated as the objects of interest, known in Croatian as the accusative case. The direct object in a sentence is generally in the accusative case. In English, the subject (nominative case in Croatian) is "he," as in "he is here" while the object (accusative case in Croatian) is "him," as in "I see him."

Knowing different cases matters in Croatian, because many of the words undergo a change as a result of the grammar being used. Each case has specific endings for nouns, adjectives, and sometimes even verbs. This sounds very complex, but don't despair. You will really only encounter and use the accusative case and those endings are provided below for your reference. Nouns in Croatian also have gender—another thing not used in English. You can spot this easily, though. Masculine nouns end in a consonant, neuter nouns end in *o* or *e*, and feminine nouns end in *a*. **Pivo** is then neuter, and **jabuka** is feminine. When ordering food or buying tickets to go somewhere, you only need to think about endings when the noun is feminine. With these feminine nouns (ending in *a*) you change the *a* (nominative case) into a *u* (accusative case). Let's take a look at a couple of examples:

Pula (*nominative feminine*)   **pivo** (*nominative neuter*)
Ja ću ići u Pulu. (*accusative*)   **Ja ću pivo.** (*accusative*)
I will go to Pula.   I will take a beer.

	Singular	Plural
Masculine	any consonant **prozor**	*-ovi/-evi* or *-i* **prozori**
Feminine	*-a* **kartica**	*-e* **kartice**
Neuter	*-o* or *-e* **selo, polje**	*-a* **sela, polja**

Nouns: Accusative Case Examples

		Accusative	
	Nominative Singular	Singular	Plural
Masculine	**prozor**	No change **prozori**	*-o(e)ve* or *-e* **prozore**
Feminine	**kartica**	*-u* **karticu**	*-e* **kartice**
Neuter	**selo, polje**	No change **selo, polje**	*-a* **sela, polja**

Note the pattern from the above two charts. The only two changes involve masculine gender (plural) and feminine gender (singular).

	Nominative		Accusative	
	Singular	Plural	Singular	Plural
Masculine	–	*-i*	–	*-e*
Feminine	*-a*	*-e*	*-u*	*-e*
Neuter	*-o/e*	*-a*	*-o/e*	*-a*

Now you can just make the connection between what you want and how to say it with the correct grammatical ending. The quick rule of thumb to remember is that if you see an *a* change it to a *u*; otherwise, do nothing. Pretend that you are starring in a mafia movie and Robert DeNiro just turned to you and said, "Aye, you!"

There are several prepositions that use the accusative case that you can employ during your trip. For example, if you want to buy a ticket to Split, you would tell the clerk at the station, "**Ja ću ići u Split**" (*ya chew ee-chee oo Split*) "I am going to Split" (literally, "I will go to Split"). The word *u* is a preposition meaning "to," and it requires the use of the accusative case, just as the word *za* is a preposition (governed by the accusative case) meaning "for." So, if you want to go to Opatija, you would change the above example to "**Ja ću ići u Opatiju**" (*ya chew ee-chee oo o-paht-ee-you*) "I am going to Opatija." Alternatively, you can say, "**Ja ću jednu kartu za Opatiju**" (*ya chew yed-knew car-too zah o-paht-ee-you*) "I will take one ticket for Opatija."

The rules that you learned above apply here in the same way.

Accusative prepositions denoting motion:
za – "for" (as in [leave, depart] for someplace)
u – "to" (an enclosed space or event, city, or country)
na – "to" (an island, peninsula, other non-enclosed space or event)

Examples

Ja ću dvije karte za Dubrovnik.
(ya chew dvee-ay car-tay zah dew-brove-nick)
I will take two tickets for Dubrovnik.

Dajte mi jednu kartu za Zadar.
(die-tea me yed-knew car-too zah zah-dar)
Please give me one ticket for Zadar.

Molim Vas, idemo na Mljet.
(mo-lihm vahs, ee-dem-mo nah me-lee-et)
Please, *[a ticket]* we are going to Mljet *[Island]*.

Genitive Case

Probably the most common but most difficult case to master is the genitive. The frequency of and reasons for its use confound even some native speakers of Croatian; but for you, this case can be broken down very simply. The case, when used without any prepositions, corresponds most commonly to possession—"of" in English. It is also used as the default case after almost 80 percent of all prepositions.

The genitive case is used when dealing with numbers, aspects of time, and ordering something such as apple juice—in Croatian, literally "juice from apples"—**sok od jabuke**. The genitive case is also used by many prepositions, but again, you do not need to know most of them to navigate Croatia during your trip.

The genitive case endings are rather simple: remember from above that **jabuka** is a feminine noun because it ends with *a*. The genitive case changes that *a* into an *e*, while for masculine and neuter the genitive ending is *a*.

Nouns: Genitive Case

	Nominative Singular	Genitive Singular	Genitive Plural
Masculine		*-a*	*-ova/-eva* or *-a*
	prozor	prozora	prozora
Feminine		*-e*	*-a*
	kartica	kartice	kartica
Neuter		*-a*	*-a*
	selo	sela	sela

The genitive case is also used when numbers are involved (recall the example above about tickets to Dubrovnik). The numbers 2, 3, and 4 all require the use of genitive singular endings. So if you want to order *two colas*, that equates to **dvije kole** in Croatian. For the numbers 5 and above (with certain exceptions, but nothing that will be encountered on a trip), genitive plural endings are used; thus, *five colas* becomes **pet kola**.

You may have noticed that with **dvije kole** both words ended with an *e*, while with **pet kola** the endings are different. This is because the number 2 behaves like an adjective. Another number that behaves like an adjective is the number 1. The only difference is that with the number 1, the genitive case is NOT used. You would instead use the accusative case.

For a more substantive list of numbers see page 223.

Examples

one cola	**jednu kolu**
two, three, four colas	**dvije / tri / četiri kole**
five colas	**pet kola**
one coffee	**jednu kavu**
two, three, four coffees	**dvije / tri / četiri kave**
five coffees	**pet kava**
one Schwepps	**jedan Schwepps**
two, three, four Schwepps	**dva / tri / četiri Schwepps-a**
five Schwepps	**pet Schwepps-a**
one meat	**jedno meso**
two meats	**dva mesa**
two tickets	**dvije karte**
six tickets	**šest karata**

VERBS

In Croatian, verbs are conjugated—that is, they have different endings depending on who is performing the action of the verb.

Verbs: I would like / I will order

I will order	**Ja bih / ću**	we will order	**mi bismo / ćemo**
you will order	**ti bi/ ćeš**	you (*formal*) will order*	**Vi biste / ćete**
he/she/it will order	**on/ona/ono bi / će**	they will order	**oni/one/ona bi/će**

*The formal *you* (i.e., sir or madam) is meant for people older than you or people who you are not familiar with. In any case, if you are unsure, just use this **Vi** form, which covers formal address and plural as in *you guys* (for plural, it will not be capitalized.)

The verb *biti* "to be"

I am	**Ja sam**	we are	**mi smo**
you are	**ti si**	you (*formal*) are	**Vi ste**
he/she/it is	**on/ona/ono je**	they are	**oni/one/ona su**

The verb *jesti* "to eat"

I eat	**Ja jedem**	we eat	**mi jedemo**
you eat	**ti jedeš**	you (*formal*) eat	**Vi jedete**
he/she/it eats	**on/ona/ono jede**	they eat	**oni/one/ona jede**

The verb *piti* "to drink"

I drink	**Ja pijem**	we drink	**mi pijemo**
you drink	**ti piješ**	you (*formal*) drink	**Vi pijete**
he/she/it drinks	**on/ona/ono pije**	they drink	**oni/one/ona piju**

The verb *imati* "to have"

I have	**Ja imam**	we have	**mi imamo**
you have	**ti imaš**	you (*formal*) have	**Vi imate**
he/she/it has	**on/ona/ono ima**	they have	**oni/one/ona imaju**

SUMMARY

Ordering food in Croatian is easy despite the overall difficulty of the grammar and the complexities of typical dialogues. There are two basic ways of ordering and only a few rules to remember.

1. I will take – **Ja ću**
2. For me – **Za mene**

The only time that the noun endings will change is if the word is feminine. If it ends in an *a* it changes to *u* for accusative case, or it remains unaltered if it is the subject.

Examples:

For me pizza.	**Za mene pizza/pizzu.**
For her a cappuccino.	**Za nju capuccino.**
For him fish.	**Za njega riba/ribu.**

Sample Dialogue:
You and your significant other enter a restaurant and take a seat.

Waiter:	**Izvolite.**	Yes, can I help you?
You:	**Za mene kola.**	For me a Coke.
Waiter:	**Dobro, a za Vas.**	OK, and for you?
You:	**Za nju espresso.**	For her an espresso.
Waiter:	**Još nešto?**	Anything else?
You:	**Ja ću pljeskavicu a ona će zelenu salatu.**	I will have a pljeskavica and she will have a lettuce salad.
Waiter:	**Može.**	Very well.

Several minutes later:

Waiter:	**Izvolite.**	Here you are.
You:	**Hvala.**	Thank you.
Waiter:	**Molim. Dobar tek!**	You're welcome, enjoy!

If you want to plunge further into the Croatian language, you will need to buy a language book, dictionary, or better yet, look for a class at a local college or cultural club. Nonetheless, we hope that this short guide helps! Other useful titles available from Hippocrene Books include:

Aida Vidan & Robert Niebuhr, *Beginner's Croatian*.
Ante Šušnjar, *Croatian-English/English-Croatian Dictionary and Phrasebook*.

Chapter 4

Getting Around in Croatia

General Tips on Traveling

Croatia is a relatively safe country. There are no documented cases of kidnappings, assaults, or any other kind of violence against tourists. But the golden rule for every traveler includes neither displaying large amounts of cash nor leaving anything unattended, even when only using the restroom. Tourist season is pickpockets' season as well, but normally only unprepared and careless tourists are victims of theft. Nevertheless, mind your valuables, especially in crowded areas such as markets.

While hitchhiking is not common in Croatia, tourists on the coast or the islands may decide to take hitchhikers with them, but as with anywhere be careful whom you take with you or which car you agree to hop into.

In this chapter we will provide you with information on Croatian public and private transportation. As most of the schedules of public transportation are subject to frequent changes, please take a look at the Web sites provided, contact the Croatian Tourist Offices, or ask at the help desk at the local boat, train, or bus stations.

Air Travel

The standard word for airport in Croatian is **zračna luka** (*zrach-nah lou-kah*), although you might also see **aerodrom** (*air-oo-drome*) on some signs, particularly in Zagreb.

There are many international flights connecting Croatia with other large European cities, and with the success of low-cost carriers such as Wizz (www.wizzair.com), Ryan Air (www.ryanair.com), InterSky (www.intersky.biz), and Sky Europe (www.skyeurope.com), flight connections are abundant and relatively inexpenisve. There is therefore no excuse for missing out on a visit to Croatia.

The most important direct international connections include those to and from Amsterdam, Berlin, Brussels, Budapest, Düsseldorf, Frankfurt, Hamburg, Helsinki, Istanbul, Lisbon, London, Mostar, Munich, Paris, Prague, Rome, Sarajevo, Skopje, Vienna, and Zurich.

Useful Web Sites

www.airport-brac.hr
www.airport-dubrovnik.hr
www.airportmalilosinj.hr
www.airport-pula.hr
www.croatiaairlines.hr
www.osijek-airport.hr
www.rijeka-airport.hr
www.split-airport.hr
www.zadar-airport.hr
www.zagreb-airport.hr

BUS TRAVEL

The bus transportation system in Croatia is great. There is hardly any place you cannot reach by bus. Many of the Web sites on bus connections do offer information in English or German, but if you can only find information in Croatian refer to this word list for help in navigating your way either through a bus station or a Web site:

(main) bus station	**autobusni kolodvor** *(ow-toe-boose-knee co-load-vore)*
arrival(s)	**dolazak (dolasci)** *(doe-lah-sack [doe-lah-see])*
(main) train station	**kolodvor** *(co-load-vore)*
choose the date	**odaberite datum** *(ode-ah-bear-eat-ay dah-tomb)*
departure(s)	**odlazak (odlasci)** *(ode-lah-sack [ode-lah-see])*
destination	**odredište** *(ode-red-eash-tay)*

point of departure	**polazište** *(poe-laze-eash-tay)*
station	**postaja** *(poe-sty-ah)* / **stanica** *(stan-eatsa)*
search, look for	**traži** *(trah-zhee)*
timetable	**vozni red** *(voze-knee red)*

Bus stations are good points to recuperate from a long trip and use the restroom and purchase some snacks and drinks. The prices tend to be a bit higher than normal, but not much. Generally speaking, buses will not have a functioning toilet onboard, so for a long ride, use the stop wisely.

At the Zagreb Airport, Croatian Airlines operates a comfortable and inexpensive bus service from the airport to the main bus terminal downtown. This option saves a tremendous amount of money compared to a taxi service, and its Web site and others are listed below.

Central bus station Dubrovnik: www.libertasdubrovnik.hr
Central bus station Split: www.ak-split.hr
Central bus station Varaždin Tours: www.ap.hr
Central bus station Zagreb: www.akz.hr
Croatian Airlines bus service: www.plesoprijevoz.hr
Croatian Bus Network: www.croatiabus.hr
Varaždin Tours: www.ap.hr
Makarska Tours: www.promet-makarska.hr

Train Travel

Take a look at the Web site for the Croatian train network before traveling by train: http://www.hznet.hr.

The most important connections from Zagreb are:

Zagreb – Maribor (Slovenia) – Graz – Beč (Beč – Vienna, Austria)
Zagreb – Budapest (Hungary)
Zagreb – Oštarije – Gospić – Knin – Zadar (Knin – Perković – Split)
Zagreb – Oštarije – Rijeka – Pula
Zagreb – Beograd (Serbia)
Zagreb – Ljubljana (Slovenia) – Venice (Italy)

While train travel is popular and well organized, the connections move at a snail's pace. The standards of cleanliness are also improving, but with a few exceptions (most notably the connection to Ljubljana, Slovenia) the trains do not meet first-class expectations. Despite this, train travel is inexpensive, allows for flexibility in travel, provides more room than buses, and permits more and heavier baggage. Here are a few terms you should know when traveling by train:

backpack	**ruksak** *(rook-sack)*
bag	**torba** *(tore-bah)*
suitcase	**kofer** *(coo-fur)*
compartment	**kupe** *(coup-ah)* (train)
luggage	**prtljaga** *(purrt-lee-agah)*
men	**muški** *(moosh-key)*
place/seat	**mjesto** *(me-ess-toe)*
platform	**peron** *(pay-roan)*
reservation	**rezervacija** *(rez-er-vat-sea-ah)*
ticket office	**šalter** *(shal-ter)*
ticket	**karta** *(car-tah)*
toilet	**zahod/toalet / WC** *(za-hoad / toe-ah-let / vee-say)*
train	**vlak** *(vlah-ck)*
train car	**vagon** *(vah-gun)*
waiting area	**čekaonica** *(check-ah-one-eat-tsa)*
women	**ženski** *(zhen-ski)*

INTRACITY TRAVEL: TAXIS, TRAMS, AND BUSES

Taxis

As already noted, taxi service in Croatia is generally very expensive. Be advised that taxi drivers will try to solicit their services at key points of travel—namely, at bus and train stations. Most of the taxi drivers know enough English to get you to your destination without problems. The majority of taxis operate with a meter and will record the trip and the transaction amount and give a receipt. But other taxis operate without a meter; we advise you not to patronize these taxis for a number of reasons, safety being foremost. You would be getting into a car with a stranger who is accountable to no one, and this could be especially risky at night.

Trams / Trolley Cars

The only two cities in Croatia that offer intracity rail transport are Zagreb and Osijek. The system in Zagreb is comparable to most major cities with mass transit. The system in Osijek is limited and unless you have a particular liking for riding on trolleys, this system can be avoided. In Zagreb, by contrast, trolleys are inexpensive and the system covers virtually any and every place in the city. The system of ticketing is rather uncommon for Americans, though.

A ticket for the tram can often be purchased from the driver or at any of the kiosks scattered throughout the city. The price at these kiosks is generally a bit lower, but not substantially. There is a machine located in the front and rear of each tram, designed to validate the ticket. You will also notice that few people actually use these machines. This is for two reasons: The first is that many people have monthly passes, which they may or may not choose to show the driver upon embarking. The second reason is that many people ride the tram illegally—that is, they do not purchase tickets. Because the trolley can be boarded without paying, the trolley network employs roving ticket "policemen" who check all passengers for a validated ticket or current pass. While the system of checking is on the rise, this is still a hit-or-miss phenomenon. We encourage you to obey all laws and regulations on your trip, but do not be surprised if a man or woman in a blue jacket asks you for your ticket (**karta** *car-tah*).

Tram ticket

City Buses

City buses function much the same as the trolleys. They have an excellent number of routes and provide service for a very modest price. The same rules regarding ticketing on trams apply here, too, but the driver often has more control over access and egress; a free ride is therefore the exception rather than the rule.

One of the major points of service for buses in Zagreb is behind the main railway station. But getting there can be difficult for those unfamiliar with the setup. The trick is to walk underground into the Importanne Centar, a popular shopping mall that goes completely under the railroad station and out to the southern side of the city. Walk down the stairs, make a left, and walk straight out to take one of the buses or walk to the southernmost part of the downtown area.

DRIVING AND CAR RENTALS

Croatian policemen are very strict, and there are severe fines against corruption, so do not try to bribe the police if stopped for any reason. While stories about corruption in Eastern Europe are prolific, do not take a chance on finding out whether the officer who has stopped you is dishonest. Major reforms have been put in place in Croatia over the last decade, and while some corruption naturally still exists, it is far from typical. The fines, by American standards, are minimal in any case, and you will be on your way in a few moments if by chance you are stopped. Some American travelers have also no doubt heard horror stories of tourists who have been stopped or approached by the "police" only to realize that criminals pretending to be police officers just made off with their valuables. While the authors have no experience of this nor have they ever heard any stories emanating from Croatia, it is still worth mentioning: the police should never ask you for your bags or anything of monetary value—if one does demand your bags, ask for his superior or call the police yourself.

Speed limits (unless otherwise posted):
50 km/h in residential areas
90 km/h in nonresidential areas
130 km/h on motorways

Other general rules:
Turn on your headlights both night and day.
The use of seat belts is obligatory.
Do not drive after you have been drinking (there is zero tolerance).
Do not use your mobile phone while driving.

In case of a breakdown, call the Croatian Automobile Club (HAK) +385 1 46 40 800 (www.hak.hr).

In case of an accident, call the police by dialing **92**, and if needed, the fire department at **93** and an ambulance at **94**.

For information about the highways, including new sections that might have recently opened, check www.hac.hr.

Because of the arid climate in parts of Croatia, be sure not to throw a cigarette butt or any other smoldering object out of the vehicle.

Car Rentals in Croatia

There are well-known international car rental companies all over Croatia, especially in the major cities and along the coast. In addition, some Croatian car rental agencies offer services throughout the country. The pricing and service should be more or less in the same range, regardless of the agency you pick. In addition, along the coast it is common to rent scooters or bikes. Check local signs and ask in the tourist office of your summer place of residence.

Avis: www.avis.hr

Dubrovnik:	Airport, 7 a.m.–9 p.m., +385 20 773811
	Hotel Excelsior, Frana Supila 12, Mon–Sat: 8 a.m.– 8 p.m., Sun: 8 a.m.–12 a.m., +385 91 3143010
Makarska:	Hotel Meteor, Kralja Petra Krešimira Iv, bb, Mon–Sat: 8 a.m.–8 p.m., Sun: 8 a.m.–12 a.m., +385 91 3143015
Opatija:	Aci Marina Icici, Liburnijska Cesta bb., Mon–Sat: 8 a.m.– 8 p.m., Sun: 8 a.m.–12 a.m., +385 (0)913143012
Pula:	Airport, Valtursko polje 210, Mon–Sun: 8 a.m.–8 p.m., +385 91 3143014
	Riva 14, Mon–Sat: 8 a.m.–8 p.m., Sun: 8 a.m.–12 a.m., +385 52 224350

Rijeka:	Airport, Riva 22, Mon–Sun: 8 a.m.–8 p.m., +385 51 311135
	Riva 8, Mon–Sat: 8 a.m.–8 p.m., Sun: 8 a.m.–12 a.m., +385 51 311135
Split:	Airport, Mon–Sun: 7 a.m.–9 p.m., +385 91 3143011
	Aci Marina, Uvala Baluni bb, Mon–Sat: 7.30 a.m.–8 p.m., Sun: 8 a.m.–12 a.m., +385 21 322689
Zadar:	Airport, Zemunik Donji, Mon–Sun: 8 a.m.–8 p.m., +385 23 205862
Zagreb:	Airport, Mon–Fri: 7 a.m.–11 p.m., Sat–Sun: 8 a.m.–11 p.m., +385 1 6265190
	Hotel Sheraton, Kneza Borne 2, Mon–Sat: 8 a.m.–8 p.m., Sun: 8 a.m.–12 a.m., +385 1 4676111

Budget Rent a Car: www.budget.hr

Dubrovnik:	Airport, Mon–Sun: 7 a.m.–9 p.m., + 385(0)20/773 290
	Obala Stjepana Radića 24, Mon–Fri: 8 a.m.–8 p.m., Sat: 8 a.m.–2 p.m., + 385(0)20/418 998
Karlovac:	Zrinjski trg 4, Mon–Fri: 8 a.m.–5 p.m., Sat: 8 a.m.–1 p.m., + 385(0)47/615 405
Osijek:	Kapucinska 39, + 385(0)31/211 500
Poreč:	Obala bb, Mon–Fri: 8 a.m.–3 p.m., Sat: 8 a.m.–1 p.m., + 385(0)52/451 188
Pula:	Airport, + 385(0)52/218 252
	Cararrina 4, Mon–Fri: 8 a.m.–7 p.m., Sat: 8 a.m.–1 p.m., + 385(0)52/218 252
Rijeka:	Trg 128. Brigade Hrvatske vojske 8, Mon–Fri: 8 a.m.–7 p.m., Sat: 9 a.m.–2 p.m., + 385(0)51/214 742
Šibenik:	Trg P. Šubića 1, Mon–Fri: 8 a.m.–3 p.m., Sat: 8 a.m.–1 p.m., + 385(0)22/216 761
Slavonski Brod:	Trg pobjede 29, Mon–Fri: 8 a.m.–5 p.m., Sat: 9 a.m.–2 p.m., + 385(0)35/448 598, 597
Split:	Airport, Mon–Sun: 7 a.m.–9 p.m., + 385(0)21/203 151
	Trumbićeva obala 12, Mon–Fri: 8 a.m.–8 p.m., Sat: 8 a.m.–2 p.m., + 385(0)21/399 214, 398 220

Varaždin:	Trg Kralja Tomislava 7, Mon–Fri: 8 a.m.–7 p.m., Sat: 9 a.m.–2 p.m., + 385(0)42/211 455
Zadar:	Branimirova obala 1, Mon–Fri: 8 a.m.–5 p.m., Sat: 9 a.m.–2 p.m., + 385(0)23/313 681
Zagreb:	Airport, Mon–Sun: 7 a.m.–9 p.m., + 385(0)1/6265 854 Praška 5, + 385(0)1/4805 688, 689 Hotel Sheraton - Kneza Borne 2, Mon–Sat: 7 a.m.– 8 p.m., + 385(0)1/4554 936, 943

Rent a Car Gramdin: www.gramdin.hr

| Zagreb: | Vladimira Preloga 5 |

Hertz Rent a Car Hrvatska: www.hertz.hr

Cavtat:	Hotel Croatia, Frankopanska 10, +385 20 475 495, Mon– Fri: 8 a.m.–12 a.m., 5 p.m.–8 p.m., Sat: 8 a.m.–11 a.m., Sun: 9 a.m.–11 a.m.
Dubrovnik:	Airport, +385 20 425 000, Mon–Sun: 8 a.m.–10 p.m. F.Supila 9, +385 20 425 000, Mon–Fri: 8 a.m.–8 p.m., Sat: 8 a.m.–1 p.m., Sun: by reservation
Hvar:	Riva bb, +385 21 742 743, summer only
Malinska:	Obala 49, +385 51 869 002, Mon–Sun: 8 a.m.–8 p.m. Obala Kralja Tomislava 15a, +385 91 414 55 05, Mon–Fri: 8 a.m.–12 a.m., 5 p.m.–8 p.m., Sat: 8 a.m.–11 a.m., Sun: 9 a.m.–11 a.m.
Osijek:	Gundulićeva 32, +385 31 200 422, Mon–Fri: 8 a.m.– 12 a.m., 5 p.m.–8 p.m., Sat: 8 a.m.–1 p.m., Sun: by reservation
Porec:	Aldo Negri 1, +385 91 310 86 91, Mon–Fri: 8 a.m.– 12 a.m., 5 p.m.–8 p.m., Sat: 8 a.m.–1 p.m., Sun: by reservation
Pula:	Airport, +385 52 210 868, by reservation Hotel Histria, Verudela bb, +385 52 210 868, Mon–Fri: 8 a.m.–12 a.m., 5 p.m.–8 p.m., Sat: 8 a.m.–1 p.m., Sun: by reservation

Rijeka:	Airport, +385 51 311 098, by reservation
	Rijeka, Riva 6, +385 51 311 098, Mon–Fri: 8 a.m.–
	12 a.m., 5 p.m.–8 p.m., Sat: 8 a.m.–1 p.m., Sun: by
	reservation
Rovinj:	c/o Hotel Park, I.M. Ronjigova bb, +385 91 4155 055,
	Mon–Sat: 8 a.m.–11 a.m., 6 p.m.–9 p.m., Sun:
	9 a.m.–12 a.m.
Split:	Airport, +385 21 895 230, Mon–Sun: 8 a.m.–10 p.m.
	Tomića stine 9, +385 21 360 455, Mon–Fri: 8 a.m.–
	12 a.m., 5 p.m.–8 p.m., Sat: 8 a.m.–1 p.m., Sun: closed
Zadar:	Airport, +385 23 254 301
	Vrata Sv.Krševana, +385 23 254 301, Mon–Fri: 8 a.m.–
	12 a.m., 5 p.m.–8 p.m., Sat: 8 a.m.–1 p.m., Sun: by
	reservation
Zagreb:	Airport, +385 1 4562 635, Mon–Sun: 8 a.m.–9 p.m.
	Vukotinovićeva 4, +385 1 48 46 777, Mon–Sat: 8 a.m.–
	8 p.m., Sun: 8 a.m.–12 p.m.

H&M Rent a Car: www.hm-rentacar.hr

Dubrovnik:	Airport, +385 20 773 239
Osijek:	Županijska ul. 8 (in the Waldinger hotel), +385 31 200 016
Split:	Airport, +385 21 203 478
Zagreb:	Grahorova 1, +385 1 370 45 35
	Airport, +385 1 622 82 63

M.A.C.K. Concord Rent a Car Service: www.mack-concord.hr

Cavtat:	Hotel Croatia, +385 20 412 732, +385 98 320-91
Dubrovnik:	Frana Supila 3, +385 20 423 747, +385 98 320 915
	Airport, +385 20 412 732
Split:	Hotel Split; Put Trstenika 19, +385 21 303 008,
	+385 98 601 727
Trogir:	Airport, +385 98 601 727
Zagreb:	Airport, +385 1 4562 385; +385 98 360 042
	Hotel Laguna, Kranjčevićeva 29, +385 1 3694555;
	+385 98 485770

FERRIES AND BOATS

Croatia has many islands that are, of course, very important for summer tourism. Therefore, the network of ferries and boats is very well organized.

Here are some useful and important words you may need for island hopping in regard to different types of water transport.

ship (does not carry cars)	**brod** *(brode)*
express ship	**brzobrod** *(brr-zoe-brode)*
ferry (carries cars)	**trajekt** *(trah-yeckt)*
catamaran (does not carry cars)	**katamaran** *(cat-ah-mah-ran)*
pier	**pristanište** *(pris-tan-eash-tay)*
harbor	**luka** *(lou-kah)*
express boat (without cars)	**hidrogliser** *(heed-row-glee-sere)*

By far the largest operator of ferries and ships is the Croatian line Jadrolinija. If you spend even a half hour at the coast, you are sure to see at least one ship from this company. Service on the various boats is relatively inexpensive, comfortable, and relaxing. Check out www.jadrolinija.hr for more information.

Jadrolinija ferry in port

The Italian Connection: Connect between Venice (Italy) and Croatia

BlueLine, online booking: www.bli-ferry.com, Ancona (Italy) – Split/Hvar/Vis
Jadrolinija, Riva 16, Rijeka: +385 51 666 111, www.viamare.com, most
destinations in Croatia.
Larivera Lines: (+39) 087582248, www.lariveralines.com, Termoli (Italy)
Korčula/Lastovo/Hvar
Miatours, Vrata sv. Krsevana, Zadar: +385 23 254 300, +385 23 254 400,
www.miatours.hr, Ancona (Italy)/Božava/Zadar/Sali/Zaglav
SNAV: (+39) 0712076116, www.snav.it, Ancona (Italy) – Split, Pescara
(Italy) – Hvar
Venezialines, Call Centre Italy and Overseas at (+39) 041 24 24 000,
9 a.m.–6 p.m., www.venezialines.com.

National Lines

Jadrolinija, Riva 16, Rijeka: +385 51 666 111, www.jadrolinija.hr, most
destinations in Croatia, check their Web site.
SplitTours: +385 21 352 533, Mon–Fri: 8 a.m.–8 p.m., Sat–Sun: 8 a.m.–
3 p.m., www.splittours.hr, Ancona (Italy) – Milna, Supetar (Brač)/
Rogač, Stomorska (Solta) – Vis – Split.
Lošinjska plovidba: Mali Lošinj, Privlaka bb, +385 51 231 524,
www.losinjplov.hr, Brestova (Istra) – Porozina (Cres), Valbiska (Krk) –
Merag (Cres).
Mediteranska plovidba: Korčula, Foša 2, +385 20 71 11 56, www.medplov.hr,
Orebić (Pelješac) – Korčula.
Rapska plovidba: Hrvatskih branitelja domovinskog rata 1/2 Rab, +385 51
724 122, www.rapska-plovidba.hr, Rab-Pag, Jablanac (Coast) – Rab.
G&V line: Renata Garbin, Moluntska 2, Dubrovnik, +385(20) 436-990,
+385(91) 4272462, www.dubrovnik4u.com/garbin/gv.html,
Zadar – Iž – Rava.
Uto Kapetan Luka: Poljička cesta 28, Krilo Jesenice, +385 21 872 877,
+38591 205 9886, +385 91 768 2085, www.krilo.hr, Korčula –
Hvar – Split.

PART II
Where to Go

Chapter 5

Zagreb

Population: Approx. 850,000
Claim to Fame: The Upper Town

Today's population of almost 1 million truly makes Zagreb (*zah-greb*) a metropolitan center where you can find or do almost anything. As tourism increases each year from across Europe and from North America, all of the services in Croatia are becoming more modern, tourist friendly, and generally more expansive. In Zagreb, you can go skydiving, eat at popular American fast-food restaurants such as Subway and McDonalds or at five-star restaurants, or find a rap or rock concert at a college student dormitory.

Opera Zagreb

Since the war in Croatia ended in 1995, Zagreb has been the site of continued economic expansion and renovation, though the greatest progress has taken place since the year 2000. The entire downtown area has become the home to high-rent apartments and businesses, including upscale shops featuring the most famous and popular brands, nestled among international corporate buildings and hotels.

The architecture of the downtown area of the city is similar to that of cities in central Europe, while the outskirts of the city speak to Zagreb's experience with communism for almost four decades of the last century. The various works of art located within the many museums of Zagreb also illustrate the rich history the city has enjoyed for almost a millennia.

Zagreb became a city during the eleventh century, when Hungarian influence reigned supreme in the northern Balkans. During this early time, Zagreb—then called Kaptol (*cap-toll*) and Gradec (*grah-dets*)—served as an outpost against attacks from roving tribes. For the next several hundred years, Zagreb increased in size and importance; with an increased ecclesiastical and military presence, the city became the recognized center of Croatia. But only in 1621, under Austrian control, was Zagreb really given an important role in Croatian political life. It was at this time that Nikola Frankopan, viceroy of Croatia (*Ban* in Croatian), made Zagreb the seat of his duchy. Slightly later, in 1669, a university was granted to the Jesuit Academy of Zagreb. Over several centuries it has functioned as the primary institute of higher education in Croatia and today is known as the University of Zagreb, with thirty-three schools of study.

Like most other budding cities of that era, Zagreb suffered terrible hardships and losses from the plague and fires. Despite this, Zagreb was rebuilt and continued to grow. While certain historic buildings were lost, redevelopment brought about a dramatic reorganization of the city. The legacy of this reconstruction is apparent in the Zagreb of today. In the city center you can get lost in the beauty of the Austrian-inspired architecture of the seventeenth, eighteenth, and nineteenth centuries, the ornate decorations and sophisticated accoutrements on the façades of many downtown locales. New meets old as these wonderful buildings are continually updated with modern technology such as satellite television and centrally controlled climate systems.

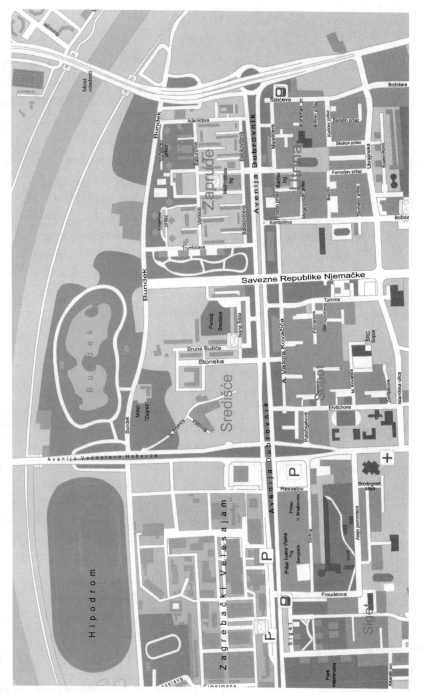

Novi Zagreb and the outskirts of town (COURTESY OF ZAGREB TOURIST BOARD)

Another aspect of new meeting old in today's Zagreb is the clash between the old architectural styles and the socialist-era paradigms that predominated during the large-scale building boom in the 1960s and 1970s. If you have a chance to venture outside of the main downtown area into **Novi Zagreb** (*novy zah-greb*; "New Zagreb"), you will be astounded by the stark differences. High-rise apartment buildings with hundreds of units constructed side-by-side are utterly identical. The government planners designed these buildings with strict attention to practicality; this is clearly evident in the extensive network of commercial establishments servicing the residential behemoths. Some buildings are so large that they contain every imaginable service establishment: a grocery store, drug store, hair salon, daycare center, post office, café, restaurant, and maybe even a variety store. Redundancy in services—prevalent in all of the former socialist countries of eastern Europe—is unavoidable in this style of city planning. Thankfully, the main tourist centers are free from such monotonous eyesores.

Because Zagreb is the metropolitan center of Croatia, the possibilities for entertainment are enormous. The markets, the large international exhibitions, and numerous cinemas, theaters, shops, churches, sporting opportunities, and the university would require at least a year or two to explore in depth. But since you probably only have a few days, you have to choose. Do you want to focus on the sights and the museums or relax along the sleepy streets over a cappuccino? We have outlined several different "tours" that you can follow in Zagreb, designed to provide a quick look at some of the best that Zagreb has to offer. But do not limit yourself to the tours—we encourage you to mix and match to best satisfy your individual tastes.

While you can do the typical tourist stuff, do not forget that Croatia is a real country inhabited by real people, and that the best experiences sometimes come from unexpected sources. Feel free to approach people on the streets and ask questions. You can practice some Croatian or simply look for young people who might speak a foreign language.

During the walking tour of Zagreb, you will see signs indicating the locations of the most prominent city monuments and museums. A rather recent addition to the city's landscape, these signs are a welcome improvement for the tourist because they provide a clear and quick way to navigate the streets without studying a map and searching for street names. The signs also help keep you on track with what you want to see so you don't forget something.

Now is also a great time to visit Zagreb because the city officials have put into motion a dynamic plan to renovate and freshen-up the city, with particular emphasis on the old city. Despite their pervasive presence throughout the downtown area, the construction projects will not disrupt a visit to Zagreb. The goal of the renovation is to brighten up the city and restore the many beautiful buildings built during the centuries of Hapsburg rule.

The main square in Zagreb is simply called **trg** (*terg*, "square") by the locals, because everybody knows the real name: **Trg Bana Jelačiča** (*terg*

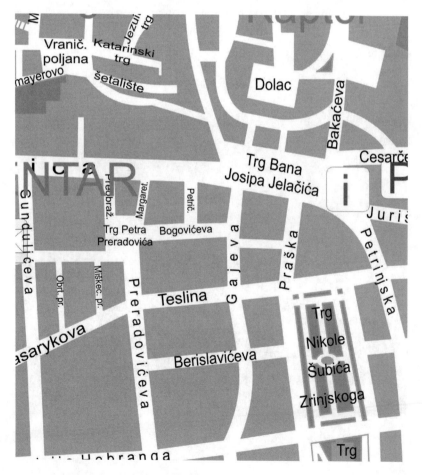

Center of Zagreb (Courtesy of Zagreb Tourist Board)

bahn-ah yell-ah-cheech-ah). This is the main meeting place for everybody during the day and at night, especially at the clock—**kod sata** (*cod sah-tah*)—where dozens of people wait for friends, businessmen meet their foreign partners, and tourists mingle; there are in fact so many people that sometimes it is hard to find the person you are looking for.

On the trg you will also find the main **tourist information office** in Zagreb, which you should visit to find additional, up-to-date information about Zagreb. Do not be shy to ask in Croatian, "**Što mogu pogledati?**" (*shtoe moe-goo poe-glea-dah-tea*; "What can I visit?"), but everybody there can help you in English.

We recommend at least three days to tour Zagreb. Below are some suggestions for tours that still cover the most important sights if you have less time.

The clock at Trg Bana Josipa Jelačić

GETTING THERE

The Zagreb airport is located to the south of Zagreb and is well connected to the city center. For information on international/national flight connections consult www.croatiaairlines.hr and www.zagreb-airport.hr. You may of course use a taxi to get downtown, but beware of very high prices; a convenient alternative is a regular bus connection operated by Croatia Airlines. For more on this connection take a look at www.plesoprijevoz.hr. Address: Zračna luka Zagreb d.o.o., Pleso bb, 10150 Zagreb.

Zagreb's main bus station (**Autobusni kolodvor** *auto-boos-knee coe-load-vore*) and main train station (**Glavni kolodvor** *glav-knee coe-load-vore*) are located very close to each other and are connected by several local trams, including number 6. From the bus station to the train station or downtown, take tram 6 labeled **Črnomerec** and get out at the third stop; from the train station take tram 6 outbound to Sopot (and also get out at the third stop).

International and intranational buses arrive at the central bus station in Zagreb, located at Av.Marina Držića 4. For more information, refer to www.akz.hr.

The most important bus connections to Zagreb include the following:

Zagreb – Beč, Südbahnhof – Vienna, Southern Station (Austria)
Zagreb – Venicija (Venice, Italy)
Zagreb – Beograd (Belgrade)
Zagreb – Sarajevo
Zagreb – Karlovac – Rijeka – Opatija – Pula – Rovinj
Zagreb – Karlovac – Poreč – Novigrad – Umag
Zagreb – Zadar – Biograd – Šibenik – Primošten – Trogir – Split
Zagreb – Karlovac – Plitvička Jezera – Zadar
Zagreb – Karlovac – Split – Dubrovnik
Zagreb – Osijek
Zagreb – Varaždin

International and intranational trains arrive at the central train station in Zagreb, located on Trg Kralja Tomislava. For more information, refer to www.hznet.hr.

Main train station in Zagreb

The most important train connections from Zagreb are the following:

Zagreb – Maribor (Slovenia) – Graz – Vienna – Beč (Austria)
Zagreb – Budapest (Hungary)
Zagreb – Oštarije – Gospić – Knin – Zadar (Knin – Perković – Split)
Zagreb – Oštarije – Rijeka – Pula
Zagreb – Beograd (Serbia)
Zagreb – Ljubljana (Slovenia) – Venice (Italy)

For car rental information take a look at Chapter 4, pages 40–44.

ACCOMMODATIONS

Since the tourist accommodations in Zagreb are limited, upon arrival you should go immediately to the tourist office to get information on hotels, motels, pensions, or dormitories. Below is a list of possible accommodations that can be reserved in advance, categorized by distance to the city center. The tourist office is located on the main square; the people there are both helpful and know major languages such as English and German. The tourist office can provide a decent map of the city and good brochures and also publishes the latest information about what is happening in Zagreb regarding concerts, art exhibits, etc. Many locals also go there for this reliable information.

While the tourist office has information about hotels, the offerings are limited. Because of a lack of hotel rooms in Zagreb, it may be hard to find accommodations for a reasonable price, and fairs and conferences often cut into the number of rooms available. Low-budget places, especially in the center of Zagreb, should be booked well in advance.

Although some of the hotels listed below are outside of the city center or the downtown area, this does not mean that they are in a different world. Zagreb is not too big, and the travel times are also short thanks to the good public transportation system, including the vital night transportation network. For Zagreb we provide a sizable list of accommodations, but since along the coast and on the islands accommodation opportunities are nearly limitless and range from the five-star hotel to someone's extra bedroom in their house, it is simply impossible to list all the possibilities.

The following list includes the appropriate contact information for accommodations, and in boldface italics, the approximate location relative to downtown. Note also that the listing for accommodations is organized by standard quality ratings (stars).

Five-Star Hotels

The Regent Esplanade Zagreb: Mihanovićeva 1, +385 1 45-66-666,
　　www.theregentzagreb.com *downtown*
Sheraton Zagreb: Kneza Borne 2, +385 1 45-53-535,
　　www.sheraton.com/zagreb *downtown*
The Westin Zagreb: Kršnjavoga 1, +385 1 48-92-000,
　　www.westin.com/zagreb *downtown*

Four-Star Hotels

ARCOTEL Allegra: Branimirova 29, +385 1 46-96-000,
　　www.arcotel.at/allegra *downtown*

Aristos: Cebini 33, Buzin, +385 1 66-95-900 *suburbs south*
AS: Zelengaj 2a, +385 1 46-09-111, www.hotel-as.hr *downtown north*
Dubrovnik: Gajeva 1, +385 1 48-63-555, www.hotel-dubrovnik.hr
downtown
Four Points by Sheraton Panorama Hotel Zagreb: Trg sportova 9, +385 1
36-58-333, www.fourpoints.com/zagreb *downtown periphery west*
Hotel Zovko: Slavonska avenija 59, +385 1 20-40-840, www.zovko.com
downtown periphery south
International: Miramarska 24, +385 1 61-08-800, www.hotel-international.hr
downtown periphery southwest
Palace Hotel Zagreb: Strossmayerov trg 10, +385 1 48-99-600,
www.palace.hr *downtown*

Three-Star Hotels

Astoria Best Western Premier Hotel: Petrinjska 71, +385 1 48-08-900,
www.bestwestern.com *downtown*
Central: Kneza Branimira 3, +385 1 48-41-122, www.hotel-central.hr
downtown
Dora: Trnjanska 11 E, +385 1 63-11-900, www.zug.hr *downtown periphery
south*
Galerija: Pogačićeva 9, Blato, +385 1 65-42-577, www.hotel-galerija.hr
suburbs southwest
Golden Tulip Holiday: Ljubljanska avenija bb, +385 1 34-96-621,
www.hotel-holiday.hr *suburbs*
Hotel Dubrava: Ljubijska avenija bb, +385 1 29-60-500,
www.hotel-dubrava.hr *suburbs east*
Hotel Gaj: Jezerska ulica 24a, +385 1 38-17-222, www.hotelgaj.hr *suburbs
west*
Hotel I: Remetinečka cesta 106, +385 1 61-41-222, www.hotel-i.hr *suburbs
south*
Jadran: Vlaška 50, +385 1 45-53-777, www.hup-zagreb.hr *downtown*
Laguna: Kranjčevićeva 29, +385 1 30-47-000, www.hotel-laguna.hr
downtown periphery west
Meridijan 16: Vukovarska 241, +385 1 60-65-200, www.meridijan16.com
downtown periphery south

The Movie Hotel: Savska 141, +385 1 60-03-600, www.themoviehotel.com *downtown periphery south*

Phoenix: Sesvetska cesta 29, +385 1 20-06-333, www.hotelphoenix.com.hr *suburbs east*

Tomislavov dom: Sljemenska cesta 24, +385 1 45-60-400, www.hotel-tomislavovdom.com *on Medveščak mountain*

Vienna: Zagrebačka cesta 211, +385 1 38-62-777 *suburbs west*

Vila Tina: Bukovačka cesta 213, +385 1 24-49-204 *suburbs (stadium)*

Two-Star Hotels

Fala: II Trnjanske ledine 18, +385 1 61-11-062, www.hotel-fala-zg.hr *downtown periphery south*

Lido: Jarun bb, +385 1 38-32-837, www.lido.hr *suburbs (Lake Jarun)*

Martini: Sesvetska cesta 109, +385 1 20-02-268, www.martini.hr *suburbs east*

Naš dom: Av. Dubrava 176, +385 1 29-88-864, www.hotel-nasdom.com *suburbs east*

Paradise: Štrokinec 26, +385 1 34-64-959, www.hotel-paradise.hr *suburbs west (Center Jankomir)*

Porin: Sarajevska 41, +385 1 66-89-300, www.zug.hr *suburbs southeast*

Sliško: Supilova 13, +385 1 61-84-777, www.slisko.hr *close to main bus station*

Zagreb: Bundek bb, +385 1 66-37-333, www.hup-zagreb.hr *suburbs (Zagreb fair)*

One-Star Hotels

AB – Partners: Vlaška 68, +385 91 548-62-84, www.apartments-zagreb.tk *downtown*

Apartman Princess: Brijunska 1, +385 98 614-414 *downtown periphery southeast*

Apartman Vito: Erdödyeva 17, +385 1 46-20-076; +385 91 48-25-915 *downtown*

Apartment Marinac: Radićeva 11, +385 98 210-468 *downtown*

Apartments Adela: Lišće 14, + 385 1 29-85-024 *suburbs northeast*

Apartments and Rooms Mirna noć: Miroševečina 35, +385 1 29-83-444, www.mirnanoc.com *suburbs northeast*

Bedeković Apartments: Grškovićeva 6, +385 98 478-522, www.apartmani-bedekovic.com *downtown*

Muzar Božo (private accommodation): Jadranska 9 +385 91 540-13-00, free-zg.htnet.hr/muzar *outer center*

Buzz Backpackers Club: Đorđićeva 24, 2. kat, +385 1 48-16-748, www.buzzbackpackers.com *downtown*

Centar: Gundulićeva 43, +385 1 23-47-434, +385 95 811-54-95, www.zgcentar.tk *downtown*

Di Prom: Trnsko 25a, +385 1 65-50-039 *suburbs*

Dolac Apartment: Dolac 1, +385 98 93-59-341 *downtown*

Evistas: Augusta Šenoe 28, +385 1 48-39-554 *downtown*

Hillberg - Real-estate agency: +385 99 21-21-441, www.hillberg.hr *downtown*

Hostel Fulir: Radićeva 3a, +385 1 48-30-882; +385 98 19-30-552, +385 91 88-75-175, http://www.fulir-hostel.com *downtown*

Hostel Lika: Pašmanska 17, +385 98 561 041 *suburbs southeast*

Hotel Antunović: Ljubljanska avenija 100a, +385 1 20-41-111, www.hotelantunovic.com *suburbs west*

Ilica: Ilica 102, +385 1 37-77-522, www.hotel-ilica.hr *downtown*

Ilicki plac: Britanski trg 1, +385 1 98 419-231, www.ilicki.com *downtown*

INTACTA apartmani d.o.o. Agency: Gundulićeva 39, +385 1 48-54-266, www.intacta-apartmani.hr *downtown*

INZAGREB d.o.o. Agency: Božidara Magovca 31, +385 1 65-23-201, www.inzagreb.com

Jagerhorn: Ilica 14, +385 1 48-33-877, www.hotel-pansion-jaegerhorn.hr *downtown*

Kod kazališta: Prilaz Gjure Deželića 34, +385 98 735-771, +385 1 46-83-236, www.kod-kazalista.com

Krovovi grada: Opatovina 33, +385 1 48-14-189 *downtown*

Laterna: N. Tesle 13, +385 91 50-65-742 *downtown*

Madi: Dotrščinska 77, +385 1 29-85-310, www.smjestaj-madi.com *suburbs northeast*

Mare: Širokobriješka 29, +385 1 36-31-191, www.accommodation-mare.com
suburbs

Marija: Berislavićeva 9, II. kat, +385 1 48-72-371, +385 91 51-90-728
downtown

MGM Hostel Ltd.: III Podbrežje 3, +385 1 60-50-358,
www.backpackers-zagreb.com *suburbs southwest*

Pansion Medvednica: Slijeme bb, +385 1 45-50-737,
www.pansion-medvednica.com *on Medveščak mountain*

Pekas.info: Sermageova 9 (Kvaternikov trg), +385 91 818-18-81,
www.pekas.info *downtown*

Plitvice: Lučko bb, +385 1 65-30-444, www.motel-plitvice.hr *on highway
west*

Prenoćište Europa: Zagrebačka 191, +385 1 38-67-177,
www.motel-europa.com *suburbs west*

Twins Apartment: Dolac 9, +385 91 55-00-654 *downtown*

Vila Marija: Potočka 18, +385 1 29-17-928, www.vila-marija.info *suburbs
northeast*

Youth Hostel: Petrinjska 77, +385 1 48-41-261, www.hfhs.hr *downtown*

Youth Hostel Ravnice: Ravnice 38d, +385 1 23-32-325,
www.ravnice-youth-hostel.hr *suburbs east (stadium)*

Youth Hotel: Odranska 8, +385 1 61-91-238, turizam@sczg.hr *student
dormitory downtown periphery (open only in summer)*

Camping

Plitvice: Lučko bb, +385 1 65-30-446, www.motel-plitvice.hr *highway west*

While it may be tempting to have breakfast at the hotel—if it is offered—
take a look at Part III, starting on page 165, to see all the other tasty options!
Now let's get started with the sample tours.

TOUR 1: THE ESSENTIAL ZAGREB (CITY CENTER)

The starting point for any tour of Zagreb is the **trg** (*terg*), or the main square in Zagreb. Prior to the disintegration of Yugoslavia in the 1990s, this was called **Trg Republike** (*terg re-poob-leak-ah*), "Republic Square." When Croatia was aspiring to independence from Yugoslavia, Zagreb's leaders made sure to name their central square after a famous Croat—and who better than **Viceroy Josip Jelačić** (*yo-sip yell-ah-cheech*)?

Jelačić was born in 1801 in the city of Petrovaradin, which is now a suburb of Novi Sad, Serbia, and is also the site of one of Europe's largest music festivals (see Web site at www.exitfest.org). Jelačić was appointed Ban (a title roughly equivalent to viceroy) during the mid-nineteenth century by the Austrian emperor Ferdinand. When Emperor Ferdinand found himself on the throne of an empire in revolt during 1848–49, the imperial authorities called upon Jelačić, as the representative of the Croatian government, to

Jelačić's birthplace in Novi Sad

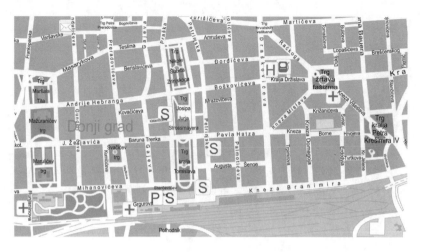

Downtown Zagreb (Courtesy of Zagreb Tourist Board)

assist in putting down the revolution in Hungary by force of arms, and he did so—successfully. Upon returning to Croatia, he abolished serfdom and ruled Croatia as a political administrator for another decade. The main sculpture at the center of the square proudly shows Jelačić on horseback with sabre in hand, no doubt in honor of his military exploits.

Also on this square you will find a little fountain, which is said to be the place where the name "Zagreb" was first mentioned. It is rumored that a local notable was thirsty and told a woman named Manduša (*man-dew-shah*) to get water for him using the verb *zagrabiti* (*zah-grab-eatie*), which translates roughly as "to scoop." But in all probability, the name Zagreb means "ditch," since the city was surrounded by water in medieval times.

Like every main square in Croatia, it has a city tavern, generically called the **Gradska kavana** (*grahd-skah kah-von-ah*), where old and young alike gossip and talk politics. Beginning the tour from the statue of Jelačić, walk west down **Ilica Street** (the street buttressing the trg) to the famous **slastičarnica** (*slah-tea-char-neat-sa*), "pastry and ice cream shop," **Vincek** (www.vincek.com.hr). Here you can get off to a good start with a coffee and some delicious sweets. After Vincek, continue farther down Ilica until you see on the right side the famous **Uspinjača** (*oos-pin-yah-cha*), which is the city's famous inclined railway.

*The Uspinjača—Zagreb's
inclined railway*

Designed originally to connect the upper and lower towns, the railway lives on as a tourist attraction. With two cabins for passengers, the line, built in the last decade of the nineteenth century, is the oldest means of mass transport in Zagreb. While not important today as a means of getting to and from work, it nonetheless transports approximately 615,000 passengers per year. The line runs from 6:30 to 9:00 every day in ten-minute intervals and charges a modest fee. You can purchase either a daily ticket or just one for a one-way trip. Enjoy the ride, because it only takes fifty-five seconds! Now that you have reached the top of the hill, the panorama of Zagreb is there for you to enjoy. On clear days, you can even catch a nice glimpse of **Novi Zagreb** across the river. Nearby, at the top of the upper town, prepare yourself for the big shot at 12 o'clock coming from the **kula** (*coo-lah*) "tower," called **Lotrščak** (*loet-rsh-chak*), located near the upper railway station on **Strossmayerovo šetalište**. From this historic tower, a blank shot is fired as part of a tradition of warning the city's residents of danger; a practice that began when the Ottoman Turks threatened the city and continued as a way to scare away thieves.

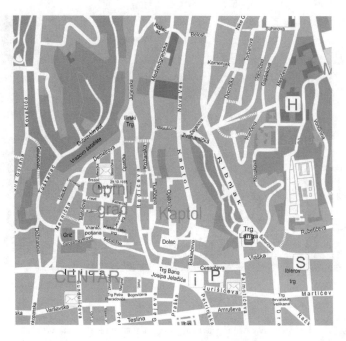

Zagreb's Upper Town (Courtesy of Zagreb Tourist Board)

Almost the entire **upper town** is a historic site with buildings dating from the seventeenth century, including Zagreb's oldest high school, the famous **Crkva Svetog Marka** (*sirk-vah svey-toag mahr-kah*), **St. Mark's Church,** and various government buildings all around the church. You will see a few inconspicuous guardposts with some policemen guarding both the Croatian Parliament—**Sabor** (*sah-bore*)—and the president's official residence. Walk around this upper town area to see the **Croatian Institute of History,** the **Greek embassy,** and some other great old buildings from centuries past. There are also a few hidden cafés in this area, which provide a unique atmosphere for you to enjoy a coffee or a midday beer.

Because this area is small, you can easily walk around in an hour or so. You are sure to pass the **Kamenita vrata** (*kah-men-eat-ah vrah-tah*) "stone gate" during your stroll in this area. Take note of it and use this way to walk out of the upper town. The history of the Kamenita vrata dates from feudal times when it was part of a stone gate leading into the upper town. When fire ravaged the area in 1731, much to the amazement of the

Entrance to Kamenita vrata

city's population, a wooden part of the structure adorned with the Virgin Mary and other holy relics survived the blaze. This miracle has been recognized ever since by people who come to the wall to light candles, pray, and offer thanks to the mother of God with plaques attached to the wall with inscriptions such as **"Hvala ti majko!"** (*qual-ah tea mai-koe*) "Thank you Holy Mother!"

Follow the stairs down past the Kamenita vrata and you will see a small square adorned with flowers, a statue, and a pleasant array of renovated buildings from centuries past (one of which today houses the **Hungarian Cultural Center**). You will see a small gap in the buildings; that is a passageway that goes into one of the most important tourist streets in Zagreb—**Tkalčićeva** (*tkahl-che-chay-vah*)—which is home to some small shops and boutiques but also has several dozen bars and cafés, including the most popular among tourists and ex-patriots, **Oliver Twist**.

Be sure to get a seat outside and observe the thousands of people who will pass by—some only once, while many others stroll by many times in search of friends or the right café to spend a nice summer afternoon. In any case, take a moment to look over the next few paragraphs to decide which major sites to visit during the remainder of your essential Zagreb tour.

The famous Tkalčićeva Street

A statue commemorating **Marija Jurić Zagorka**, the first female journalist and popular novelist, is located on Tkalčićeva. This monument by the sculptor **Marija Ujević-Galetović** is simple and discreet, but her historical impact should not be overlooked. Born in the late nineteenth century, Zagorka was the founder of the *Woman's Journal* (*Ženski list*) and wrote prolifically on contemporary issues facing both women and all Croats, including discrimination and efforts to undermine Croatian cultural distinctiveness. As an advocate for Croatia's rights, she has lived on as a testament to Croatia's quest for a sovereign identity. Although, unfortunately, it is difficult to find her works in English, some progress is currently underway toward making her impact on Croatian history better known. For a short sample of one of her works, entitled the *Secret of the Bloody Bridge,* go to http://germslav.byu.edu/perspectives/2005/Woods_K.pdf.

From Oliver Twist, following Tkalčićeva up the hill, you will reach Zagreb's most trendy high-end shopping mall, complete with posh cafés and restaurants. On the weekends, the most fashionable of Zagreb's youth come to parade and flirt. In addition to such brand-name stores as Hugo Boss, there is a multiplex cinema and a host of international restaurants. Coming

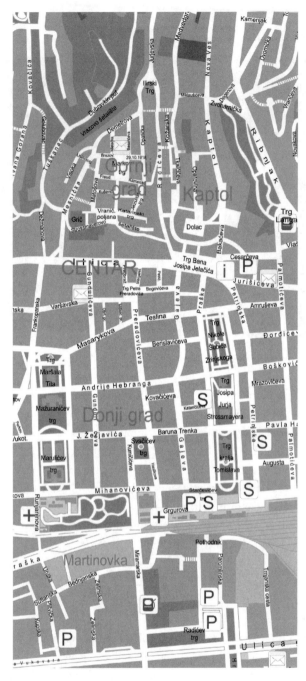

Central Zagreb (Courtesy of Zagreb Tourist Board)

Zagreb Cathedral

back down Tkalčićeva, to the left of Oliver Twist, is a long stairway leading down to **Kaptol ulica** (*cap-toll oo-leat-sah*). Go down the hill (to the right) and pass several great tourist-friendly restaurants as well as street vendors selling souvenirs and gifts. At the end of this trek, you will see the spectacular **Zagreb Cathedral**.

The main cathedral has a history dating back over seven hundred years. Inside the cathedral lie holy relics from the eleventh century, the same time period when the Zagreb bishopric was founded. Even the late Pope John Paul II held services here. Currently under restoration, the beauty of the cathedral is still visible, but some of its most important treasures lie in the cultural significance of the **glagoljica** (*glah-goal-eat-sah*) "Glagolitic letters," found on the inside walls. Glagolitic letters were used by various Slavic speakers in the Balkans as an alphabet before either the Cyrillic or Latin alphabets were available to most literate people (for more, check out www.croatianhistory.net). Photography is permitted inside the cathedral, and the statues and ornate artwork are magnificent.

Behind the cathedral is **Ribnjak Park** (*rib-knee-ak*), a nice natural space for sitting and enjoying either hot summer weather or a cool and breezy autumn with the changing colors of the trees.

Any essential tour of Zagreb would be incomplete without a look at the outdoor market—the **Dolac** (*dough-lots*). Here you can find an endless variety of fruits and vegetables, along with other homemade foods like cheese. Use this opportunity to grab a few sweet grapes on a hot summer day and don't be shy about trying some before you buy. Fish and meat can be found downstairs, and you can treat yourself to a special brandy or **rakija** along the edges of the open-air market. Nearby the Dolac are old women selling handicrafts such as lace tablecloths and coasters along with fresh flowers and other trinkets.

Useful Phrases

May I try?	**Mogu li probati?** *(moe-goo lee pro-bah-tea)*
Good, sweet!	**Dobro, slatko!** *(doe-bro slat-koe)*
Half a kilo, please.	**Molim Vas, pola kile.** *(moe-lim vas, poe-lah key-lah)*

Finally, the heart of Zagreb comes to an end with the **Krvavi most** (*curve-ah-vee moast*) "bloodbridge," the site of the ancient border between the two towns that merged to form Zagreb. One of the bloodiest confrontations between the feuding denizens of the two towns is commemorated on this wooden bridge, which crossed the **Medveščak Creek**. The Medveščak is now gone, replaced by **Tkalčićeva**, and the only surviving relic of the feud is by the bridge. From here, walk southward back to the trg and prepare for another exciting trip in Croatia's capital.

By this time, you are sure to be hungry and one of the most important things in Zagreb is finding a great place to eat. We have provided a short listing of restaurants in Zagreb, most of them complete with more information online, but because of the rapid changes underway in Zagreb, we hesitate to make specific comments on them. Skip ahead to the end of this chapter for this listing (page 80), but for tips on choosing the perfect place to eat, take a look at Chapter 11, Going to a Restaurant (page 181).

TOUR 2: ADDITIONAL ZAGREB

As with the first tour, the starting point is again the trg, but this time you will visit the part of Zagreb that is to the south, where the terrain is flat. This tour offers a nice view of the downtown area complete with parks, cafés, and museums.

Starting from the southwest corner of the trg, head south along the pedestrian path that leads to a big fountain across from the **Hotel Dubrovnik** and the Subway restaurant. At the fountain, turn right. You will be walking past a host of cafés with plenty of outside seating—sometimes too much outside seating, because when it is full during nice days, it can be difficult to maneuver through the crowd or find an empty table. You will see numerous shops along this street in addition to cafés and straight ahead is a cinema. At this point, you will see the major Orthodox Church in Zagreb located on **Preradovićev trg** (*prey-rad-oh-vee-chev terg*). This was built by the city's former Serbian population and, unlike in other areas during the wars in the 1990s, the church remained largely untouched and still remains a center of activity for the small Serbian community.

You can stop at any of the fashionable stores located in and around this trg but be sure to head south and then turn at **Masarykova ulica** (*mass-*

Trg Maršala Tita in Zagreb

are-ee-coe-vah ool-eatsa). Follow this street and at the end is a great view of some of the most prominent buildings in the city. At this point you are on **Trg Maršala Tita** (*terg marr-shal-lah tea-tah*), "Marshal Tito's Square," and can see the **law school** and **university administration building** to the right (http://rektorat.unizg.hr/homepage), the **Croatian National Theater** to the left, the **Croatian Museum of Education** directly in front of you (written as the **Hrvatski školski muzej**) and a bit of the famous gallery **Mimara**. This important trg is still named after Tito, who ruled former Yugoslavia for thirty-five years as a communist dictatorship. Walk past the theater (the large, yellow building) through the garden. Check to see if any signs advertise any upcoming performances and if so, go to the main door and see if the ticket office is open. The lawn of the theater is nicely manicured and several recent statues have been added representing various figures from Croatian history and culture. You can also check their Web site for any upcoming events or performances at www.hnk.hr/en/repertoar.php.

Another large building directly south of the theater also boasts a series of attractive gardens. In the direct vicinity lies the ethnographic museum, **Etnografski muzej** (check out www.mdc.hr/etno/eng for more). This museum displays a host of various trinkets transcending the ages. Tools, handicrafts, furniture, folk costumes, musical instruments, religious objects, and more are displayed there alongside loan exhibitions from other major ethnographic museums.

Next you come to the **Mimara Museum**, which displays world-renowned art and is home to numerous touring exhibitions from museums from across the globe. It was opened in 1987 and houses almost four thousand works of art in a wide range of styles and materials and culture of origin. If you were to only visit one museum in Zagreb, this is it!

Moving further south still, you will pass the **Croatian State Archives**, marked only by a small sign on the wall, buried on the face of the pleasant nineteenth-century building behind a spacious garden. Directly across from the archive building to the south is the city's **botanical garden**. The entrance is not apparent at first glance, but walk along the length of **Mihanovićeva ulica** (*me-han-o-vea-cheva oo-lea-tsa*) and you find a discreet gate with a sign giving the working hours. While the botanical gardens do not feature flora from around the world, the garden is nonetheless a nice collection of plant life arranged in a pleasant manner.

Exiting the gardens, continue east past a new hotel-casino and past the **Glavni kolodvor** (*glave-knee coe-load-vore*), "train station." Unlike many stations that tend to be sleazy, the Zagreb train station has been recently renovated and truly looks first class. Directly on the square at the station is a statue to **King Tomislav**, the first Croatian king.

This area is so clean and attractive because it serves as a shopping and transportation hub for Zagreb. There are always open taxis to be found in front of the station, which also serves as a point of transit for many of the trams. While waiting for one, you can look over the numerous magazines, flowers, handmade lace, and sometimes souvenirs. Down below is the **Importanne centar** (*impor-tan-nay cen-tar*), a mixture of cafés, eateries, supermarkets, variety stores, and small boutiques.

Walking north away from the train station and the statue of Tomislav, you will find the **Umjetnički paviljon** (*uhm-yet -neach-key pah-vill-ion*), "art

Statue of King Tomislav I in Zagreb

pavilion." Built about a century ago, this building stands directly across from and faces the train station. Its sole purpose has been to house artistic works, but on the ground floor there is an entryway leading to a formal restaurant. The museum is worth a visit and the exhibits are always changing thanks to good connections with other museums in the region. Check out the Web site to see which artist or theme is on display during your visit: www.umjetnicki-paviljon.hr.

Continuing on to the north, you will encounter another park area with the address of **Strossmayerov trg** (*stross-meyer-ove terg*). It is named after the famous Croatian politician and Catholic theologian of Austro-Hungarian times. Born in Osijek to descendents of mixed Croatian and German heritage, Strossmayer served in several major positions in the government and theological hierarchy as a result of his good relationships with Emperor Franz Josef, Ban Jelačić, and Pope Pius IX. The park features an attractive display of gardens and various statuettes. Parallel to the park is the **former embassy of the United States**, the current **Ministry of Education**, and in the adjacent park, **Zrinjevac** (*zrin-zeah-vats*), you will see one of the most important courts of the government of Croatia.

At this point in the tour take a quick stroll down **Teslina ulica** (*tes-lean-ah oo-lea-tsa*), named after the famous inventor Nikola Tesla, one of the pioneers of modern electricity, who after achieving international fame with his inventions went to the United States and worked until his death. Some of the pleasant tourist shops and boutiques that adorn this street are well worth a quick visit before heading north, back to **Trg Bana Jelačića**.

Congratulations! You have finished another tour of Zagreb and in the process have seen many of the most notable sites the city has to offer. Take a look at Tour Number 3 for more interesting sites outside the boundaries of a walking tour.

TOUR 3: FURTHER POINTS OF INTEREST

While a tour of additional sites of interest would be possible, these are spread out throughout the city and there is no logical itinerary that links them. As a result, the following sites are listed in no particular order—simply pick and choose which features you would like to see.

Maksimirski Park

For nature lovers, **Maksimirski Park** (*max-ee-meer-ski*) offers a little of everything—from a small lake to benches where you can watch birds. If the weather is right, you can also picnic here on one of the grassy pastures. The best way to get here is from the trg using tram numbers 4, 7, 11, or 12, getting out at **Bukovačka** (*bouk-oh-vach-kah*) and walking farther east until you encounter the park. Spread across both sides of the street, Maksimirski is also home to a major soccer stadium and is near the **Zoološki vrt grada Zagreba** (*zo-oh-losh-key vert grah-dah zah-grey-bah*), Zagreb's city zoo, which was founded in 1924 and offers all of the typical exhibits of a medium-size zoo.

Echo chamber in Maksimirski Park

Art Center

Built originally to commemorate the great Croatian artists Julije Klović
and Ivan Meštrović, the art center now located at the **Trg žrtava fašizma**
(*terg zher-tah-vah fah-sheeze-ma*), "Square of the Victims of Fascism," was
home to Zagreb's Muslim population during World War II. As a mosque,
the building changed little aside from the addition of three minarets, which
also were not there for long. The postwar government under Tito ordered the
minarets removed and made the center into a museum of the People's Revolution. During the 1990s, the nature of the sight changed again, and it is now
once more an art museum.

Mirogoj Cemetery

Getting to the cemetery will take only a few minutes; it is most easily reached
by bus—the number 106 from **Kaptol** ("cathedral"). This cemetery does not
make any distinction between the faiths of the occupants. As a result, you
can find Catholic, Orthodox, and Jewish graves intermingled throughout

Mirogoj cemetery

the cemetery. Structured like a park and rich in architecture, sculptures, and inscriptions, a trip to this otherwise mournful spot is worth your time. The graves of many important people in Croatia's history, such as the first Croatian president, Franjo Tuđman (May 14, 1922–December 10, 1999), are located here. Visit www.gradskagroblja.hr for more information.

Velesajam

The **Velesajam** (*vela-sai-am*) is home to the international exhibition hall for conventions such as auto shows, trade fairs, and major sporting events. Check the Web site (www.zv.hr/index_en.html) to see if there is an event of interest taking place. Take tram number 7 to Savski Most or 14 to Zapruđe, and then exit at the Velesajam stop.

Džamija (Mosque)

While few Croats practice Islam, enough Muslims reside in Croatia to warrant several mosques. Most of these are located in villages and are increasingly frequent closer to the Bosnian border. The **Džamija** (*jam-ee-ya*) is the major mosque in Zagreb, located in Novi Zagreb, and is home to a large and vibrant Muslim community. But since it is newly constructed, the mosque has neither Byzantine-era mosaics nor a rich history. The easiest way to get there is to take tram number 7 to Savski Most and get off when you see the minaret.

The "Big" Market

The big market at **Jakuševac** (*yak-oo-shay-vats*) takes place on Sundays and, to a limited extent, on Wednesdays. To reach this large, open-air market, take bus number 295 from the main station or tram 7 to Savski Most and get off right after you cross the river. From this point, walk east along the river and you will see the crowd of thousands of Croats trading new and used goods.

The market is a haven for all that Croats wish to get rid of; fortunately for tourists, you can see the flavor of the Balkans packed into a few small acres. You can buy antiques—including Communist-era paraphernalia—pirated music and movies, old books and magazines, and even a car! There is always something new and exciting going on at the market, and some of the most colorful stories of a visit here might come about at one of the many food stands located at key points in the market area. These small restaurants offer traditional Croatian foods such as ćevapi (*che-vap-ee*) and pljeskavica (*plea-es-kah-vea-tsa*) and serve all of the common soft drinks and Croatian beers that help wash down the greasy—shall we say "stodgy"—meats and breads. If there is a funny smell in the area, that is normal—a major city landfill is nearby.

Museum of Contemporary Art

The name says it all in regard to this museum. While the first modern Croatian art appeared with the work of Josip Siessel in 1922, modern art did not catch on in Croatia until after World War II. The museum thus caters to the wide varieties of modern art that have been popular since the 1960s. Check out www.mdc.hr/msu and look for signs saying **Muzej suvremene umjetnosti** for more information.

Croatian Naïve Art Museum

Naïve art is an art form unique to the twentieth century, for it combines the lack of training typical among amateur artists with a distinctly earthy style and down-home expressionism. This type of art has thrived in Croatia, and as a result, Croats have constructed some of the most prized pieces. The museum—called in Croatian the **Hrvatski muzej naivne umjetnosti**—is located on **Ćirilometodska ulica** 3 (*cheer-ill-o-me-toad-skah oo-lea-tsa*), and is open from Tuesday to Friday, 10 a.m.–6 p.m.; Saturday and Sunday, 10 a.m.– 1 p.m. Check out the Web site for more information: www.hmnu.org.

City Museum

The **Gradski muzej** (*grad-ski moo-zay*), "Museum of the City of Zagreb," houses over 4,500 objects, and although it serves as the primary municipal museum for Zagreb, there are also more general Croatian pieces on display. The museum catalogs the history of the city from the earliest known times until the present day. Accompanying the permanent exhibit of various objects is a working wood shop, engaged in the preservation of various antique pieces. The museum is located on **Opatička ulica** 20 (*o-pat-each-kah oo-lea-tsa*) and is open from Tuesday to Friday, 10 a.m.–6 p.m.; Saturday and Sunday, 10 a.m.– 1 p.m. More information about recent and upcoming special events is available at www.mdc.hr/mgz.

Useful Vocabulary

Here is a list of the most important words you may need to understand Croatian Web sites, especially for the clubs that offer different programs during different seasons. To navigate the Web site, just search for **vijesti** (*vee-yeah-stee*), "program," or **novosti** (*know-vost-tea*), "news."

Months of the Year

	Abbreviation	Pronunciation	Translation
Mjeseci		*me-ace-et-see*	months
Siječanj	Sij	*see-yeah*	January
Veljača	Velj	*vel-ya-chah*	February
Ožujak	Ožu	*oo-zhoo-yak*	March
Travanj	Tra	*trah-vahny*	April
Svibanj	Svi	*svee-bahny*	May
Lipanj	Lip	*lee-pahny*	June
Srpanj	Srp	*sir-pahny*	July
Kolovoz	Kol	*co-low-voaz*	August
Rujan	Ruj	*rou-yahn*	September
Listopad	Lis	*lees-toe-pahd*	October
Studeni	Stu	*stew-den-ee*	November
Prosinac	Pro	*pro-seen-ats*	December

Days of the Week

	Abbreviation	Pronunciation	Translation
Nedelja	Ne	*nay-dell-yah*	Sunday
Ponedjeljak	Po	*po-nay-del-yak*	Monday
Utorak	Ut	*oo-tour-ak*	Tuesday
Srijeda	Sr	*sree-ed-ah*	Wednesday
Četvrtak	Če	*chet-ver-tak*	Thursday

	Abbreviation	Pronunciation	Translation
Petak	Pe	*pay-tak*	Friday
Subota	Su	*sue-bow-tah*	Saturday
Radni dan		*raad-knee dahn*	working day
Blagdan		*blahg-dahn*	holiday

BARS AND CLUBS

BP Club: Teslina 7, www.bpclub.hr
Dublin Pub: Maksimirska 75, Wed.–Sun., www.dublinpub.hr
Gapclub: F. Andraseca 14, 8 p.m. –4 a.m.
Gjuro 2: Medveščak 2, Tue.–Sat., http://gjuro2.hr
Global Club: P. Hatza 14, 9 p.m. –
Hemingway: Tuškanac 1, www.hemingway.hr
KSET: Unska 3, www.kset.org
The Movie Pub: Savska 141, Mon.–Wed.: 7 a.m.–2 a.m., Thur.–Sat.:
7 a.m.–4 a.m., Sun.: 9 a.m.–2 a.m., www.the-movie-pub.com
Purgeraj: Park Ribnjak 1, click on *Kaj ima* (*kai ee-mah*) – "What's up," to
get the program, www.purgeraj.hr
SAX!: Klub hrvatskih glazbenika, Palmotićeva 22/2, www.sax-zg.hr
Tvornica: Šubićeva 2, Café 8 a.m.–10 p.m., Club 10 p.m.–4 a.m.,
www.tvornica-kulture.hr

RESTAURANTS

This is a brief list of restaurants and Web sites with guides to restaurants in
Zagreb. Please note that this information changes rapidly, and an Internet-
based search may yield different results.

www.index.hr/gastro/gdjejesti
www.gastronaut.hr
www.zagreb-touristinfo.hr

General Restaurants

Bistro Jadera: Zeleni trg 4, +385 1 6055 250, Mon.–Sat.: 8 a.m.–11 p.m., www.jadera.hr

Gallo Restaurant: A. Hebranga 34, 12 a.m.–12 p.m., www.gallo.hr

Ivica i Marica: Tkalčićeva 70, 12 a.m.–10 p.m., www.ivicaimarica.com

Karaka: Andrije Hebranga 12, +385 1 48 17 150, Mon.–Sat.: 11 a.m.–11 p.m., www.karaka.hr

Kerempuh: Kaptol 3 – Tržnica Dolac

Kpivovari: Ilica 224, www.kpivovari.com

Okrugljak: Mlinovi 28, 11 a.m.–1 a.m., www.okrugljak.hr

Pivnica Medvedgrad Adžijina: – Božidara Adžije 16, Pivnica Mali Medo Tkalčićeva – Tkalčićeva 36, Pivnica Medvedgrad Samoborska – Samoborska Cesta 217, www.pivnica-medvedgrad.hr

Pressclub: Perkovčeva 2, Mon.–Sat.: 11 a.m.–5 p.m., www.pressclub.hr

Pri zvoncu: Vrbik 1, Mon.–Sat.: 8 a.m.–11 p.m., www.prizvoncu.com

Restaurant Boban: Gajeva 9, www.boban.hr

Restaurant Bonaca: Trakošćanska 41, 10 a.m.–12 p.m., www.restoranbonaca.hr, 10 a.m.–12 p.m.

Restaurant Hrvatski kulturni klub: Trg maršala Tita 10

Restaurant Jaegerhorn: Ilica 14, +385 1 4833 877, www.hotel-pansion-jaegerhorn.hr

Restoran Baltazar: Nova ves 4, www.restoran-baltazar.hr

Restoran i pivnica Kaptolska klet: Kaptol 5, www.kaptolska-klet.hr

Restoran kod Pavela: Gračanska cesta 46, http://kodpavela.ipo.hr

Ribarski Brevijar: Kaptol 27/1, +385 1 48 29 999, Mon.–Sat.: 12 a.m.–1 a.m.

Stari fijaker: Mesnička 6, +385 1 48-33-829, 7 a.m.–11 p.m., Sun.: 10 a.m.–10 p.m.

Vinodol: Teslina 10, 10 a.m.–12 p.m., www.vinodol-zg.hr

Zagorcu: Frankopanska 13, +385 1 48-30-538, 10 a.m.–12 p.m., Sun.: 10 a.m.–7 p.m.

Italian Restaurants

Bistro Capuciner: Mon.–Sat.: 10 a.m.–1 a.m., Sun.: 12 a.m.–1 a.m.,
    Kaptol 6, +385 1 4810 487, +385 1 4814 840, www.capuciner.hr
Restoran Maslina: Stupnička 14, +385 1 61 91 225, www.maslina.hr
Restoran Placa: Radićeva 42, Mon.–Fri.: 11 a.m.–10 p.m.,
    +385 1 48 13 390, www.placa.hr

Croatian National Cuisine

Lido: Jarun b.b., +385 1 38 32 837, www.lido.hr
Medvedgrad (Castle at Medveščak): 12 a.m.–10 p.m.; closed Mon.,
    +385 1 45-56-226 Restoran
Miramare: Miramarska 19, Mon.–Sat.: 7 a.m.–11 p.m., +385 1 6110-732,
    www.miramare.hr
Restaurant Medvednica: Bukovačka 4, 8 a.m.–12 p.m., +385 1 24-21-263,
    www.medvednica-maksimir.hr

Restaurants with Dostava *(dough-stah-vah; delivery)*

PI:PI – **Pizza i pivo: Delivery:** 10 a.m.–2 a.m., 0800 74 74
Pivnica Mlinarica: Jandrićeva 36, **Delivery:** 01/4615-999, weekdays: 10 a.m.–
    10 p.m., Sun.: 12 a.m.–10 p.m.; **dining room open:** 8 a.m.–11 p.m.,
    Sun.: 9 a.m.–11 p.m.
Rubelj Grill: "The Croatian Fast Food Chain" – **Delivery:** 9 a.m.–11 p.m.,
    +385 1 2911-411 (50kn minimum); **Restaurants:** Zagreb, Dolac 2 –
    Tržnica mala terasa, Frankopanska 2, Livanjska 23, Srednjaci, Teslička
    2 – Dubrava, Kruge 19A, Branimirova tržnica, J. Bračuna 16 – okretište
    Črnomerec, Koledinečka bb – Tržni centar Dubrava, Savska cesta 118,
    Trešnjevački trg, Šubićeva 40 – Tržnica Gorica, Barčev trg bb – Utrine
    tržnica, Ugao I. i II. Ferenščice www.rubelj-grill.hr

Vegetarian Restaurants

Ivica i Marica: Tkalčićeva 70, 12 a.m.–10 p.m., www.ivicaimarica.com
Restoran Nova: Ilica 72, +385 1 48 100 59, Mon.–Sat.: 9 a.m.–10 p.m.,
www.biovega.hr
Sirion: Boškovičeva 19, +385 1 48 17 839, Mon.–Fri.: 10 a.m.–6 p.m.,
Sat.: 12 a.m.–3 p.m., Sun. and holidays closed

OTHER SERVICES

Shopping Centers

www.branimircentar.hr
www.centarkaptol.hr
www.citycenterone.com
www.importanne.hr

Internet Cafés

@ VIP: Iblerov trg 10, Mon.–Sat.: 8 a.m.–11 p.m., Sun.: 9 a.m.–11 p.m.,
www.vipnet.hr
ART: Tkalčićeva 18, 8 a.m.–11 p.m., www.art-caffee.com
Art Net Club: Preradovićeva 25, Mon–Fri: 9 a.m.–10 p.m., Sat: 11 a.m.–
5 p.m.
Charlie Net: Gajeva 4, Mon.–Sat.: 8 a.m.–10 p.m.
Cyber Café Sublink: Teslina 12, Mon.–Sat.: 9 a.m.–10 p.m., Sun.: 3 p.m.–
10 p.m., www.sublink.hr
Ergonet: Badalićeva 26c, Mon.–Fri.: 8 a.m.–10 p.m., Sat.: 9 a.m.–10 p.m.,
www.ergonet.hr
Iskoninternet - KIC: Preradovićeva 5/I, Mon.–Sat.: 9 a.m.–11 p.m., Sun.:
12 a.m.–11 p.m., http://internetcentar.iskon.hr
Net kulturni klub mama: Preradovićeva 18 (backyard), Mon.–Sat.: 10 a.m.–
10 p.m., Sun.: 4 p.m.–10 p.m.
VIP: Preradovićev trg 5, 8 a.m.–11 p.m.

Mail

Postcards can be bought at many kiosks or at any of the tourist shops. Remember that the same postcards are found at the main post office. The central post office is located next to the central train station, which is approximately a 10-minute walk from the trg. Check out the official Web site for the Zagreb Post Office: www.posta.hr.

Cinemas

Croatian cinemas almost exclusively show foreign films, and they are almost always subtitled, so the American tourist can watch most of the movies currently playing in the United States while in Croatia. Most of the movie theaters use older technology, but some stunning examples of multiplex cinemas with the biggest and best of everything exist in Zagreb.

Broadway Tkalca: Nova Ves 11 (Centar Kaptol), www.broadway-kina.com
CineStar Zagreb: Branimirova 29, www.blitz-cinestar.hr
Croatia: Katančićeva 3, www.croatia-film.hr
Europa: Varšavska 3, www.kinematografi.hr
KIC Art: Preradovićeva 5, www.kic.hr
Studentski Centar: Savska 25, www.sczg.hr

CULTURE IN ZAGREB

Aside from the major museums, Zagreb has a lot to offer. Take a look at the short list below and then browse the Web sites of museums that might be of interest.

Museums

Archaeological Museum: Trg N. Š. Zrinskog 19, Tues.–Fri.: 10 a.m.–5 p.m., Sat. and Sun.: 10 a.m.–1 p.m., www.amz.hr
Architect Viktor Kovačić Apartment: Masarykova 21, Thur.: 10 a.m.–5 p.m., www.mdc.hr/mgz
Arts and Crafts Museum: Trg maršala Tita 10, Tues.–Fri.: 10 a.m.–7 p.m., Sat. and Sun.: 10 a.m.–2 p.m., www.muo.hr

Croatian Architecture Museum: I. G. Kovačića 37, Mon.–Sun.: 11 a.m.–
6 p.m., www.hazu.hr/ENG/Cro_Mus_Arch.html

Croatian History Museum: Matoševa 9, Mon.–Fri.: 10 a.m.–5 p.m., Sat.
and Sun.: 10 a.m.–1 p.m., www.hismus.hr

Croatian Naïve Art Museum: Ćirilometodska 3, Tues.–Fri.: 10 a.m.–6 p.m.;
Sat.–Sun.: 10 a.m.–1 p.m., www.hmnu.org

Croatian Natural History Museum: Demetrova 1, Tues.–Fri.: 10 a.m.–
5 p.m., Sat. and Sun.: 10 a.m.–1 p.m., www.hpm.hr

Croatian School Museum: Trg maršala Tita 4/I, Tues.–Fri.: 10 a.m.–5 p.m.,
Sat. and Sun.: 10 a.m.–1 p.m., closed Mondays and holidays,
www.hrskolski-muzej.hr

Croatian Sports Museum: Ilica 13, Mon.–Fri.: 8 a.m.–3 p.m.,
www.sportski-muzej.hr

Croatian State Archives: Marulićev trg 21, www.arhiv.hr

Ethnographic Museum: Mažuranićev trg 14, Tues.–Thur.: 10 a.m.–6 p.m.,
Fri.–Sun.: 10 a.m.–1 p.m., www.mdc.hr/etno/eng/index.html

Gliptoteka HAZU: Sculpture Museum of the Croatian Academy of Science
and Arts, Medvedgradska 2, Mon.–Fri.: 11 a.m.–7 p.m.; Sat. and Sun.:
10 a.m.–2 p.m., www.hazu.hr

Hunting Museum: V. Nazora 63, Wed., Fri., Sat.: 8 a.m.–1 p.m., Tues.,
Thur.: 12 p.m.–5 p.m.

Ivan Mestrović Foundation: Mestrović Atelier, Mletačka 8, Tues.–Fri.:
10 a.m.–6 p.m., Sat. 10 a.m.–2 p.m.

Kabinet grafike HAZU: A. Hebranga 1, Mon.–Sat.: 10 a.m.–6 p.m.,
www.hazu.hr

Memorial Collection of Jozo Kljaković: Rokov perivoj 4 (Likovni centar
grada Zagreba), Mon.–Fri.: 9 a.m.–1 p.m., 3 p.m.–9 p.m.;
www.likovni-centar.htnet.hr

Memorial Collection of Miroslav and Bela Krleza: Krležin Gvozd 23, Tues.:
11 a.m.–5 p.m., www.mgz.hr/eng/fs-files/krleza.html

Mimara Museum: Rooseveltov trg 5, Tues., Wed., Fri., Sat.: 10 a.m.–5 p.m.,
Thur.: 10 a.m.–7 p.m., Sun.: 10 a.m.–2 p.m.

Museum and Workshop Franjo Schneider: Trg M. Tita 11, Wed.: 10 a.m.–
1 p.m.; 4 p.m.–7 p.m., www.muzej-franje-schneidera.com

Technical Museum: Savska cesta 18, Tues.–Fri.: 9 a.m.–5 p.m., Sat. and
Sun.: 9 a.m.–1 p.m., www.mdc.hr/tehnicki/hr/

The Richter Collection: Vrhovec 38a, Wed. and Sat.: 11 a.m.–4 p.m.,
www.mdc.hr/msu

Galleries

AGM – Art Point Centar: Gundulićeva 21, Mon.–Fri.: 8 a.m.–8 p.m., Sat.: 8 a.m.–2 p.m.

Atelier Gallery ARHO: Tkalčićeva 13/II, Mon.–Fri.: 9 a.m.–8 p.m., Sat.: 9 a.m.–2 p.m.

Badrov Gallery – Photo Art Gallery: Trg žrtava fašizma 1, Fri.: 10 a.m.–2 p.m.; 4 p.m.–8 p.m., Sat.: 10 a.m.–2 p.m., www.galerija-badrov.com

Croatian Artists Centre: Trg žrtava fašizma bb, Tues.–Fri.: 11 a.m.–9 p.m., Sat., Sun.: 10 a.m.–2 p.m.

Deči Gallery: Radićeva 19, Mon.–Fri.: 9 a.m.–1 p.m.; 5 p.m.–8 p.m., Sat.: 9.30 a.m.–1.30 p.m., www.galerijadeci.hr

Forum Gallery: Nikole Tesle 16, Mon.–Fri.: 10 a.m.–2 p.m. and 4 p.m.–8 p.m., Sat.: 10 a.m.–2 p.m. www.kic.hr

Kaptol Gallery: Kaptol 13, Mon.–Fri.: 9.30 a.m.–8 p.m.

Klovicevi Dvori Gallery: Jezuitski trg 4, Tues.–Sun.: 10 a.m.–8 p.m., Fri.: 10 a.m.–10 p.m., www.galerijaklovic.hr

Lotrščak Tower: Strossmayerovo šetalište, Tues.–Sun.: 11 a.m.–7 p.m.

Mala Gallery: Trg bana J. Jelačića 6, Mon.–Fri 9 a.m.–9 p.m., Sat.: 9 a.m.–2 p.m., www.galerijamala.hr

Mirko Virius Gallery – Association of the Naive Artists of Croatia: Tkalčićeva 14, www.hd-naiva.hr, Mon.–Sat.: 10 a.m.–1 p.m. and 5:30 p.m.–8.30 p.m.

Miroslav Kraljević Gallery: Šubićeva 29, Tues.–Fri.: 12 p.m.–7 p.m., Sat.: 11 a.m.–1 p.m., www.g-mk.hr

Modern Gallery: Hebrangova 1, Tues.–Fri.: 10 a.m.–6 p.m., Sun.: 10 a.m.–1 p.m.

Mona Lisa Gallery: Tkalčićeva 77, Mon.–Fri.: 10 a.m.–8 p.m., Sat. and Sun.: 10 a.m.–2 p.m., www.galerija-mona-lisa.com

Strossmayer Gallery of Old Masters: Trg N. Š. Zrinskog 11, Tues. 10 a.m.–1 p.m. and 5 p.m.–7 p.m., Wed.–Sun.: 10 a.m.–1 p.m., www.mdc.hr/strossmayer

Ulupuh Gallery: Tkalčićeva 14, Mon.–Fri.: 9 a.m.–1 p.m. and 5 p.m.–7 p.m., Sat.: 10 a.m.–1 p.m., www.ulupuh.hr

Theaters

Croatian National Theatre: Trg maršala Tita 15, www.hnk.hr
The Dubrava Children´s Theatre: Cerska 1, www.ns-dubrava.hr
Exit Theatre: Ilica 208, www.teatarexit.hr
Gavella Drama Theatre: Frankopanska 8, www.gavella.hr
ITD Theatre: Savska 25, www.sczg.hr
Kerempuh Satirical Theatre: Ilica 31, www.kazalistekerempuh.hr
KNAPP: Ivanićgradska 41a, www.kcpescenica.hr
Komedija: Kaptol 9, www.komedija.hr
Mala scena Theatre: Medveščak 2, www.mala-scena.hr
Ribica Children's Theatre: Park Ribnjak 1, www.cmr.hr
Trešnja Municipal Theatre: Mošćenička 1, www.kazaliste-tresnja.hr
Zagreb Puppet Theatre: Trg kralja Tomislava 19, www.zkl.hr
Zagreb Theatre of the Young: Teslina 7, www.zekaem.hr
Žar Ptica Municipal Theatre: Bijenička 97, www.zar-ptica.hr

Libraries

Nacionalna i Sveučilišna Knjižnica: Hrvatske bratske zajednice 4,
www.nsk.hr

AROUND ZAGREB

The suburbs of Zagreb offer little for the ordinary tourist with limited
vacation time. North of Zagreb, though, you can find a ski slope; south of
Zagreb lies the airport where you can find skydiving opportunities, and to
the east some of the older neighborhoods exhibit an old-world charm. West
of Zagreb is the township of **Samobor**, an area popular with Zagrebers for
weekend getaways and the best **kremšnita** (check out this cream-filled dessert online at www.samoborske-kremsnite.com). In general though, the suburbs are home to most of Zagreb's population and thus consist of residential
and light commercial buildings.

Medvedgrad

One big mistake you can make in Zagreb is to confuse **Pivnica Medvedgrad** (*peave-neat-sah med-ved-grahd*) with **Medvedgrad**, "castle." The first is a beer-garden with its own brewery (www.pivnica-medvedgrad.hr) and the second is an old castle up on the hill in the north of Zagreb. Besides their name, they do have one thing in common: Both are worth seeing and better when seen right after each other.

The castle lies in the national park of **Medvednica** (*med-ved-nea-tsa*), which is situated on the Medvednica mountain. **Medved** in the local Croatian dialect means "bear," and while bears no longer inhabit the forests of Croatia, the bear still maintains a large role in Croatian folklore. The whole mountain is part of the larger region called the **Hrvatsko zagorje** (*her-vat-skoe zah-gor-yay*). On weekends, families use the tram lines and the ski lift to reach the top of the mountain, called **Sljeme** (*slee-em-may*), and then take a stroll to enjoy the fresh air and the great views of the surrounding countryside. Check out the Web site for more information: www.sljeme.hr. To get to Sljeme, take tram number 14 to Mihaljevac (*me-hail-yay-vats*) and change

Castle Medvedgrad

there to the number 15 to Dolje (*dole-yay*). Then take the **žičara** (*zhee-char-ah*), the ski lift, up to the top of Sljeme.

Samobor

With the charm of a small village, and yet only a few minutes from downtown Zagreb, **Samobor** (*sam-o-boar*) is a nice, relaxing getaway for the tourist with a car. Its small weekend houses and quaint restaurants make Samobor a lovely retreat from the hustle and bustle of Zagreb. You will also find an interesting museum in Samobor, called **Muzej Marton**, located at Jurjevska ulica 7. The opening times are Sat.–Sun.: 10 a.m.–1 p.m., and the Web site is at www.muzej-marton.hr. Samobor is also home to the famous **samoborska kremšnita**, which is a special version of the delightful creamy pastry found at bakeries all over Croatia. If you make the trip to sleepy Samobor, sit down and enjoy one of these along with a coffee.

Samobor

CHAPTER 6

CONTINENTAL CROATIA

Northeast of Zagreb

Međumurje (*med-jew-moor-yay*) is the region around the cities of Čakovec (*chak-o-vets*) and Varaždin (*var-ahz-dean*). These small cities offer an alternative for the tourist who wishes to see a bit more of Croatia than merely the coast. The area is quite intriguing, with a lot of cultural and historical sites of interest. The area takes no more than two days to explore if you travel by car. Tourist information for Međumurje can be found online at www.tzm.hr.

ČAKOVEC

Population: 16,000
Claim to Fame: Zrinski Castle

Čakovec (*chah-co-vets*) is named after Dimitrius Chaky, the court magistrate of the thirteenth-century Hungarian king Bela IV, who built a large wooden tower in the region of Međumurje. The name Čakovec, however, comes from the Hungarian word "*csháktornya*" ("Chaky's tower"). Later, a fortification was built by the tower with a permanent armed presence, and a settlement developed that eventually grew into the present city of Čakovec. The Zrinski familiy, one of the most important Croatian families in the sixteenth and seventeenth centuries, helped to develop the city and make it into a regional hub for commerce and transport. Take a walk around the city to the castle, visit the museum, and settle into one of the two most comfortable restaurants of little Čakovec: **Katarina** located at Matice hrvatske 6, or for fish try the **Riblji restoran Feral** at Kralja Tomislava 2, both approximately a one-minute walk from the main square.

Main square in Čakovec

Check out www.tourism-cakovec.hr for more information and special events.

Čakovec Highlights

Stari grad Zrinskih/Muzej – The old castle of the Zrinski family
Museum of Čakovec

VARAŽDIN

Population: 50,000
Claim to Fame: The Baroque Capital of Croatia

Varaždin (*vah-razh-dean*) is neither a large nor wealthy town. Despite these handicaps, the city is a great addition to any trip to Croatia. Accessible by bus or train from Zagreb, with regular and frequent connections throughout the day, the city is a must-see for its great contribution to Croatian culture and history. With ten art galleries, several great museums, palaces, and numerous churches, any visitor to Varaždin will immediately recognize this diamond in the rough. The old city is charming and the inner city area is packed with churches and palaces of former notables. You will find the information center in the downtown area about a ten-minute walk from the train station, directly south of **Trg M. Stančića** (*terg em stahn-cheach-ah*). The city cemetery is well-known for its park-like atmosphere as a result of eighteenth-century renovation; at that time, the city was also the center of fashionable high life in Croatia. If you are visiting on a Saturday in spring or summer, you can catch a glimpse of the changing of the city guard. This event is truly unique to the region and displays the marvelous splendor of Napoleonic-era military uniforms and garb.

The musical and artistic side of the city comes alive in summer and autumn when craftmen, artists, musicians, and their fans all gather in the streets to celebrate Varaždin's rich past.

Varaždin hosts annual music festivals (including jazz and baroque music) and thanks to the rich surrounding environment is a center for nature lovers and hunters. The biggest and most well-known event in the city, though, takes place in August and September. It's the **Špancirfest** (*shpahn-sear-fest*), a street festival offering live music, live theater, street vendors, and an overall exuberant atmosphere. The city center will be filled with **ulična glazba** (*oo-leach-nah glaz-bah*), "street music," and **ulični teatar** (*oo-leach-knee tay-ah-ter*),

Varaždin's Castle

"street theater." Check out the Web site at www.spancirfest.com for more information.

Useful Web Sites

www.apartmani-hrvatska.com
www.gastrocom.hr
www.gmv.hr
www.mdc.hr/varazdin
www.tourism-varazdin.hr
www.turizam-vzz.hr
www.varazdin.hr

Varaždin Highlights

Stari Grad (*starry grahd*) – Old Castle
Kula stražarnica (*koo-lah stah-zhar-nea-tsa*) – Watch Tower
Palača Sermage (*pah-lah-cha sehr-mah-gah*) – Sermage Palace
Lisakova kula (*lees-ah-coe-vah koo-lah*) – Lisak Tower
Vijećnica (*vee-yed-nea-tsa*) – town hall
HNK u Varaždinu (*ha-n-kay oo vahr-azh-dee-new*) – Croatian National Theatre in Varaždin
Palača Erdödy (*pah-lah-cha err-doe-dee*) – Erdödy Palace
Groblje (*globe-lee-ay*) – cemetery
Gradski muzej Varaždin (*grahd-ski moo-zay vahr-ayz-dean*) – City Museum of Varaždin

Eastern Croatia

Eastern Croatia is generally known for its relatively rich agriculture and pleasant villages scattered across the countryside. The landscape is diverse, with small rolling hills where people grow grapes and distill brandy, and flat plains perfect for large-scale agriculture. This region was unfortunately also a victim of its human diversity—during the wars in the 1990s, fighting between Croats and Serbs left some areas ravaged and barren. A great deal of money has been allocated to repairing the wartime damage, and while a lot has been accomplished, much work remains. Villages are probably the most affected—even more than a decade after the war ended—but some of the major cities also exhibit relatively severe physical damage.

Croatian village life

Croatian countryside

But the fighting and its aftermath should not discourage the tourist from going to the region. Cities such as **Osijek** (*o-see-jek*) and **Vukovar** (*vook-o-vahr*), along with the surrounding areas offer some nice views and excursions for tourists.

Check out the following Web sites for a more general overview of possible destinations: www.tzosbarzup.hr; www.tzzps.hr.

BJELOVAR, PAKRAC, AND SLAVONSKI BROD

The pleasant roadtrip experience is certainly part of what makes these towns interesting to visit. The rolling hills and the lush countryside offer good opportunities for a picnic or for photographing the panoramic scenery. Although these places are accessible via public transportation—mostly by bus—and although bus transportation is generally great in Croatia, the connection times needed and the number of stops needed to reach these towns could make for a tiring trip. **Bjelovar** (*bee-el-o-vahr*) has a quaint little downtown and a pretty suburban area where you can enjoy a nice coffee or have a hearty meal with lots of meat—something that Eastern Croatia (also known as **Slavonia**) is known for.

Pakrac (*pahk-rahts*) is a town interesting for its recent wartime history. Never a center for commerce or industry, the town remained ethnically mixed and emerged as one of the early centers for conflict when Yugoslavia began breaking apart. A point of conflict for the next few years, the town today is slowly recovering thanks to grants from government and international institutions. In front of the police station stands a monument emphasizing the shallowness of conflict and horrors of war.

Slavonski Brod (*slah-vone-ski brode*) is a major business and industrial center for the area and is the last big city along the highway from Zagreb to Belgrade, Serbia. If you are taking a long drive, this is a good place for a short rest stop and for touring the city by car or the city center on foot. Slavonski Brod lies on the border with Bosnia-Herzegovina, and across the frontier the town is called Bosanski Brod. The bus from Zagreb to Sarajevo may also pass through this area, but is unlikely to stop here.

Osijek

Population: 115,000

Claim to Fame: Fortress / Tvrđa (*tver-jah*)

Osijek (*o-see-yeck*) remains the major city in the region in regard to industry, commerce, and residential areas, including suburbs. There is also fertile agricultural land in the region thanks to the nearby Danube and Drava rivers, which flow right next to the heart of the city. Check out Chapter 9 (page 159) for more information on **Kopački rit**, a wonderful national park featuring flora and fauna specific to this area due to the flooding patterns of the Danube into the lowland-basin region, which is only minutes from Osijek.

The old city offers an enjoyable walking tour for visitors, taking in the great **Trg Svetog trojstva** (*terg svay-toag troy-stvah*), "Holy Trinity Square," the **Slavonian Museum, St. Michael's Church**, and the **New Franciscan Monastery** (founded in 1773). All of these sites are located in the old fortress complex at the eastern end of the city and are accessible by tram along **Europska avenija** (*europ-skah ah-ven-ee-ya*). The city emerged first as

Osijek's main square

a fortress as early as the late twelfth century and quickly became a key strategic point between competing kingdoms in the region. Its presence on two major rivers also made it a key point for controlling trade throughout the northern Balkans. When the Ottoman Turks attempted to move into Hungary, they first captured Osijek in 1526 and remained there for 161 years. The fortress as it is now was constructed by the Austrians. In the twentieth century, as part of a modernization program, some sections of the walls and fortifications were removed and so now you can sit along the waterfront in one of the numerous cafés.

The rest of the city offers tourists some attractive views, a relaxing atmosphere, some entertainment possibilities at the theater, several churches, and many parks that dot the cityscape.

Useful Web Sites

www.osijek.hr
www.tzosijek.hr

VUKOVAR

Population: 32,000
Claim to Fame: Most Dramatic Battle During War in Croatia in 1990s

During the first phase of the war between the Croats and Serbs, **Vukovar** (*vook-o-vahr*) became a primary target for the Serbian forces, who shelled the city endlessly and reduced it to ruins. Once the Serbian forces had taken over Vukovar, they held it for the next few years and did little with it. The pictures of the city speak for themselves regarding the devastation. While some parts of the town have been rebuilt, many of the ruins remain a testament to the cruelty of war. Bullet holes and bombed-out buildings greet those arriving by car or by Danube ferry.

Only in the last few years have Serbs begun to return and resettle in the city, but in general, the once prosperous little shipping port on the Danube now exists as a shadow of its former self.

One of the more dramatic sites of the city lies a few minutes' drive away from the center. This is the massive cemetery, the final resting place of war veterans and civilian victims. A testament to the war—Croatia's equivalent to

*Visible war damage
in today's Vukovar*

the Arlington National Cemetery—the cemetery takes about a half hour to walk through and appreciate.

The only non-war symbol from Vukovar is the **Vučedolska golubica** (*vooch-ay-dole-skah go-lube-eatsa*), the "Dove from Vučedol," which is a small village close to Vukovar. The dove is a pre-Slavic cultural piece but has become associated with Eastern Croatia because Croats have immortalized the dove in the form of a small ceramic pot, which you can buy almost everywhere— even on a rainy day in a parking lot.

Useful Web Site

www.tzvsz.hr

VINKOVCI

The last of the relatively large towns near Osijek and Vukovar is **Vinkovci** (*vin-cove-see*). With a sizeable population and large business base, the town has recovered from the war but still displays some battle scars. While some buildings are still in shambles, many others have been rebuilt or are under construction in an area previously dominated by empty land lots. A drive through the town would go well with a trip to either Osijek or Vukovar, or better still, to both of them, to get a feel for how various cities have managed to progress since conflict ended in 1995.

ILOK

Ilok (*ee-lock*) is known for its great quality wine and as the easternmost city in Croatia. On the border with Serbia, the Ilok area has four border crossings with Serbia—but be warned that only one is for foreigners; the others are for only Croats and Serbs. The city is also unique in its Islamic-inspired architecture, and while it is out of the way for the average tourist, wine lovers should not miss out on drinking some of the best wine Croatia has to offer directly from the barrel and buying a bottle or two to enjoy back home.

Western Croatia

While not known for tourism, the area generally located to the south and west of Zagreb does have a few things to offer. The city of **Karlovac** is a short drive away from Zagreb and can be reached at almost any time of the day via bus. Karlovac also serves as an important transportation hub for travelers going to the coast. It has tourist possibilities in its own right and was historically a vital piece of the military frontier between Austria and the Ottoman Empire.

KARLOVAC

Founded in 1579
Population: 60,000
Claim to Fame: Beer / Karlovačko pivo

Karlovac (*car-low-vats*) is home to more than just a brewery, since it was the historic hub for the military frontier and developed as a garrison town that, over time, expanded into a commercial and transportation crossroads serving the entire Dalmatian coast and northern Bosnia. The inner city of the town is designed in the manner of a feudal fortress, featuring a star-shaped wall. While most of this wall is gone, the logic of the downtown area still follows this historical pattern. The city has a large and pleasant park—the **Gradski park**, "city park"—located downtown, which also still displays scars of the last war in Yugoslavia, when Karlovac was on the front line. Visitors can rest assured that with festivals and special events going on year round, Karlovac is never boring. Some of the more unusual events held in this small city include an international ballroom dancing contest and an international Taekwondo tournament.

Just outside the city lies the old castle of **Dubovac,** built during the thirteenth century and offering a wonderful panorama of the city and the surrounding countryside. The city museum in the center exhibits the works of local artists in addition to city memorabilia and also features traveling shows. Art is quite important for this small city, and besides the collection at the city museum, several notable galleries and art schools also are located in the downtown area.

Typical Croatian church

Useful Web Sites

www.karlovac.hr
www.karlovac-touristinfo.hr
www.tzkz.hr/eindex.asp

Other Useful Web Sites for this Region

http://us.croatia.hr/home
www.tz-koprivnicko-krizevacka.hr
www.visit-croatia.co.uk/addresses

CHAPTER 7

THE COAST

The information on accommodations along the coast is voluminous, and long lists of places to stay have been compiled by the Croatian tourist board and private tourist agencies; you can thus get all the necessary brochures at several tourist agencies in Croatia or online. So to avoid duplicating the great information already available, we will refrain from listing the accommodation options; rather, we will give suggestions to help choose what will be best for your vacation. If you cross the Croatian border from the north by car, you will receive information pamphlets while waiting to pass through

The beautiful coast of Croatia

the border security checkpoint. These pamphlets are distributed by the Croatian Tourist Association and cover a substantial amount of up-to-date information. They can also be obtained in the major tourist offices such as the one in Zagreb, as well as—to a more limited extent—in the bus stations and train stations. And be sure to also contact the Croatian tourist board in your country.

All along the coast, wherever you are, in the smallest village or even on a hidden beach, you will find tourist offices, private accommodation agencies, and a plethora of signs for vacant rooms—just look for **camere**, **Zimmer**, **sobe**, or "rooms." In addition to these roadside signs, there will always be people, young and old alike, at the bus and train stations offering rooms for tourists. Do not be shy about these offers: typically, older women with

Rovinj

empty rooms in their homes add to their state social security by renting out rooms nightly or weekly. The prices are generally reasonable, the service usually friendly, and the cultural experience unbeatable. Keep in mind that many of these people may not know English, but things always find a way of working themselves out, and your trip will be no less enjoyable despite a language barrier.

In the unlikely possibility that you cannot find accommodations on your own, you can always spot a taxi driver or somebody in the street and ask, "**Znate li gdje ima slobodnih soba?**" (*znah-tea lee lee gah-day ee-mah slow-boad-neeh sow-bay*), "Do you know where I can find available rooms?"

Do not be surprised if the Croatian tourist agency or owners of privately operated bed-and-breakfasts tell you that apartments or rooms are only available for an entire week. That may be the case sometimes, especially if you look for accommodations on a Saturday or Sunday afternoon. During the week, short-time visitors may be more welcome—keep in mind that Croatia's primary income derives from tourism during the peak season (June–August) and a vacant room is a big loss for the landlord. If there are no rooms available at first sight, don't despair; either a landlord with a booked apartment or a travel office will be able to point you in the right direction because even during high season when the Italian summer break causes traffic jams and it seems that the entire Croatian coast is occupied, you will find a place to stay the night. This is partly thanks (strangely enough) to the legacy of communism in Yugoslavia, which allowed for and even encouraged the construction of thousands of vacation houses along the coast. Today, as a result of increasing tourism, owners are eager to rent out these houses, and with each year the standards are raised and already fully equipped houses are becoming ever more comfortable for tourists. The only downside to the accommodation varieties listed above is that generally speaking, you should not arrive late in the day or in the evening to secure a room. Typically, only hotels allow late-night check-in, and of course, a hotel might not be the most inexpensive choice if you are traveling on a budget.

One of the options for travel in the region during your stay in Croatia is a short trip to Venice. By boat, Venice is but a few hours away, and if you have not yet been there, it might be worth looking into as a brief side-trip. Many travel agencies in Istria and the Kvarner region offer (day) trips to Venice, so take a look at www.venezialines.com/eng/index.asp for more information.

Connections are available departing from Mali Lošinj, Piran, Poreč, Pula, Rabac, Rovinj, and other harbors.

While a quick trip to Venice might add variety, time is also needed to enjoy all the beauty that Croatia has to offer! As a start, this chapter outlines some of the better destinations along the famous Dalmatian coast, providing the information needed for a great seaside adventure. For an overview of the great variety of opportunities available, use an online search engine to investigate tourist agencies and popular destinations. You can also start with www.atlas-croatia.com or www.istra.hr.

Grand Canal in nearby Venice

PULA

Population: Approx. 58,500
Claim to Fame: Roman Amphitheater

Like many other coastal Croatian cities, **Pula** (*poo-lah*) was settled in the first millennia before Christ by Illyrians, followed thereafter by colonizers from Rome (called Colonia Pietas Iulia Pola). This colony of Romans clearly left its mark on the city, as seen by some of the important architecture still preserved there. When Rome fell, chaos descended upon Pula, and the city suffered wave after wave of barbarian attacks. Finally, in the seventh century, Slavs migrated to the Istrian peninsula and reached Pula.

Due to its proximity to Venice, Pula soon found itself absorbed by the Italian power. Possession by Venice brought prosperity and joy, but it also brought about the pain and devastation of conflict. Being a part of Venice meant that numerous armies swept through Pula killing, raping, and burning whatever stood in their path. After Napoleon's sweep across northern Italy, Pula, like most other Croatian cities, became a part of the Illyrian Provinces,

Roman amphitheater in Pula

but after Napoleon's defeat at Waterloo it fell under the authority of Austria. During this time the Austrians made effective use of the fantastic harbor at Pula, and the city became the naval and shipbuilding center of the Austro-Hungarian Empire. The end of World War I brought Pula back into Italy but only for a short time; the end of World War II and the dramatic Italian defeats for the first time brought in Yugoslav power. Originally under the authority of the United Nations, the entire Istrian peninsula became the center of the Cold War debate over the issue of who would gain control over Trieste and the surrounding area—Italy or Tito's Yugoslavia. While in the end, Trieste was awarded to Italy and Istria, along with Pula, went to Yugoslavia, the issue is clouded by the still-present Italian minority.

When you first enter Pula you will see the formidable **arena—the Roman amphitheater** built in the first century for gladiator fights. Today, the arena is open for public viewing, and during special occasions such as festivals or concerts, the arena hosts up to five thousand guests. If you do not make it to Pula during one of these special occasions, you can still see the coliseum; tours run daily, but individuals can also pay an entrance fee and walk around the facility unescorted. A good time for taking pictures is toward sunset, as the sunlight sifting through the columns and arches provides you with a souvenir that will last a lifetime.

Besides the amphitheater, there are numerous other sites to see while in Pula. A stroll around the old city reveals many great architectural wonders dating from Roman times to the late nineteenth century. Look toward the hilltop to see the **historical museum of Istria**, where they have a lovely collection of Austro-Hungarian naval relics—a must-see for any military history enthusiast. Although small, the hilltop museum has a lot of interesting pieces that should be of interest for an hour or so. If military history is not your forte, a visit to the **fortress** is still worthwhile for the striking view of the entire city and the local surroundings that makes for a great photograph.

Parking in Pula can be a bit troublesome, but there are two options: either find an open spot in a private pay-per-hour parking lot, or leave the car about a ten-to-fifteen-minute walk from the tourist area. If you arrive by bus, the station is only a few minutes on foot from all the sights—and from hotels. A stop in the tourist office will require some time because of the multitude of brochures and leaflets and the huge listing of accommodations throughout the city.

*Roman arch
in Pula*

Useful Web Sites

www.pula.hr
www.pula24.com
www.pulainfo.hr

Pula Highlights

Triumphal Arch of the Sergi – Golden Gate
Temple of Augustus
Floor mosaic: "The Punishment of Dirce," near the Chapel of St. Maria
    Formosa
Twin gates and city walls
Gate of Hercules
Forum
Cathedral of the Assumption of the Blessed Virgin Mary

Orthodox Church of St. Nicholas
Small Roman theater

ROVINJ

Population: Approx. 13,000
Claim to Fame: Church of St. Euphemia

Rovinj (*row-veen*) is one of the more popular and treasured seaside towns in
Istria. With a history similar to that of other Istrian towns, stretching as far
back as Roman times, you are sure to note the Italian feel of the city. Small
and compact, Rovinj lies nestled on the western coast of Istria, hiding many

*Church of
St. Euphemia
in Rovinj*

pleasant little surprises for visitors. A walk around the old city will uncover numerous churches and giant public buildings—the most famous of all being the **Church of St. Euphemia.**

In the vicinity of Rovinj, as is the case with most of the other cities in Istria, there are large complexes offering a variety of accommodations—from campsites to hotels with beachfront property. If you have a car and can explore before you book a room somewhere, take a quick drive around and see if one of these waterfront travel centers looks appealing.

Useful Web Sites

www.rovinj.info (providing more than thirty private accommodations)
www.tzgrovinj.hr

Rovinj Highlights

Grisa – pedestrian zone up the hill to the church, full of galleries and art shops
Museum of Rovinj – Trg Maršala Tita 11, ++385 52 816 720,
www.muzej-rovinj.com

OPATIJA

Population: Approx. 8,000
Claim to Fame: Palaces and Panorama

Opatija (*oo-pat-ee-jah*) is a city not to be missed, especially when visiting any part of Istria. Only a few minutes away from Rijeka, Opatija lies on the eastern coast of Istria and is known for the great views of Rijeka and sunrises over the Adriatic. Here you can take a tour of one of the many palaces in the city and the surroundings and walk along the old city, enjoying a cappuccino or a nice lunch of fresh fish. The city is known for exclusive hotels and features one of the oldest pop music competitions in Croatia (Opatijski festival).

The city is also known throughout former Yugoslavia as the home of Opatija-brand cigarettes, though the authors wish to warn any smoker away from these if you find them—fame does not always mean quality!

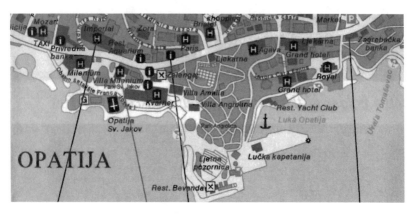

Opatija (COURTESY OF OPATIJA TOURIST BOARD)

Useful Web Sites

www.opatija.net
www.opatija-tourism.hr

Opatija Highlights

Djevojka s galebom, "The Girl with the Seagull" – Designed by Zvonka
Cara, this is an attractive statue marking the pleasantness of the
Opatijan riviera.

RIJEKA

Population: Approx. 52,000
Claim to Fame: Harbor and industry

The earliest settlers in what is today **Rijeka** (*re-ache-ah*) were members of
Celtic tribes, but these people soon fell victim to Roman colonizers. During
the decline of Rome, the city was subjected to waves of barbarian assaults
and only stabilized in 1466(!), when the Austrians took control of the city.
Called Fiume at this time to represent the city's predominantly Italian population, Rijeka eventually came under the authority of the Hungarian part of
the Habsburg monarchy and was administered from Budapest. As a result of
this political situation, Rijeka competed with Trieste as the major center for

shipping and trade both for the Austro-Hungarian Empire and for southern and eastern Europe in general.

The expansion of Rijeka as the primary port for Hungarian shipping on the Adriatic was rapid and brought great wealth to the city. Consequently, city leaders also devoted a great deal of time and money to various cultural projects. This legacy can be seen today in the famous **Cultural Center of Rijeka** and the internationally known **Croatian University** in Rijeka. Rijeka also has an American connection: before becoming mayor of New York City (1934–45), Fiorello LaGuardia lived in Rijeka while working at the U.S. consulate there. LaGuardia himself was no stranger to the Balkans because his mother's hometown of Trieste lies close to Rijeka and shares a similar cultural and political heritage.

Statue of the Girl with the Seagull, Opatija

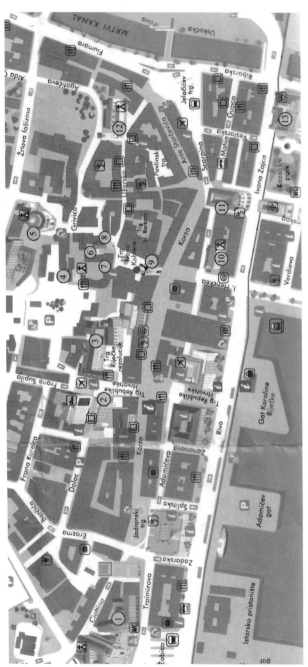

Downtown Rijeka (Courtesy of Rijeka Tourist Board)

1 – **Palača Ploech** / Ploech Palace
2 – **Sveučilišna knjižnica (stalna izložba glagolice)-Muzej moderne i suvremena umjetnosti** /
   University Library (permanent exhibition of Glagolitic script) and Museum of Modern and
   Contemporary Art
3 – **Dominikanski samostan, Crkva sv. Jeronima, ex Palača Municipija i Stendarac (stup za
   gradsku zastavu)** / Dominican Convent, Church of St. Jerome, former municipal palace and
   Stendarac (the city flagpole)
4 – **Kapela sv. Fabijana i Sebastijana** / St. Fabian's and St. Sebastian's Chapel
5 – **Katedrala sv. Vida** / St. Vitus Cathedral

6 – **Rimski luk "Stara vrata"** / The Old Gateway Roman Arch
7 – **Ostaci kasnoantičkog kastruma** / Ruins of the late-antiquity castrum
8 – **Stara gradska vijećnica** / Old Town Hall
9 – **Gradski toranj** / City Tower
10 – **Pravoslavna crkva sv. Nikole** / Orthodox Church of St. Nicholas
11 – **Palača Modello** / The Modello Palace
12 – **Crkva Uznesenja Blažene Djevice Marije i Kosi taranj** / Church of the Assumption and
   the Leaning Tower
13 – **Hrvatsko narodno kazalište Ivan pl. Zajca** / "Ivan pl. Zajc" Croatian National Theater

114

Downtown Rijeka

The period following the end of World War I brought confusion over which country should rule Rijeka—Italy or Yugoslavia. Both countries laid claim to the city because there were a significant number of both Italians and Croats living there. The site of various military occupations and coups, the city of Rijeka was taken over by Italy while the hinterland was retained by Yugoslavia (then known as the Kingdom of Serbs, Croats, and Slovenes). This arrangement supposedly ensured that the ethnic groups would not be ruled by foreigners; inevitably, however, any such settlement in the Balkans that is based on ethnicity is of dubious value. In Rijeka and elsewhere, the Italian state tried to "Italianize" the Croatian population through forced education in Italian and a mandatory adoption of Italian-sounding last names. As a result, it is easy to find Croats named Mario or who have Italian surnames. With Italy on the losing side at the end of World War II, Rijeka once again came up for grabs; in the end, the new Yugoslavia held on to Rijeka and redeveloped it into the primary port city of the country. Today, in addition to the many small craft and private vessels, fishing brigs, large passenger cruise ships, and commercial tankers and cargo ships are often crowded together in port.

One of the major spectacles that has made Rijeka famous in modern times for tourists is the Catholic festival known as **Carneval**. The old city comes alive, and at night thousands of people don costumes and roam the streets, creating a citywide party that turns Rijeka into the New Orleans of Croatia. If you plan on coming during this time—generally February or March—reserve accommodations far in advance because the city will be full. The festivities last for several days, and visitors are never disappointed.

Rijeka has many worthy tourist attractions aside from Carneval. The geography of the city, with the lowland area directly on the water's edge and the steep slopes reaching to the top of the mountains, means that seeing everything requires some uphill walking. Many of the tourist-friendly sites, however, are located along the water's edge—along the harbor, the outdoor market, and finally near the main pedestrian avenue—and can be seen during an hour-long stroll. Don't miss the market for a glimpse of the fresh fish, fruits, and vegetables, combined with standard market fare such as clothes, perfume, and magazines. The market is right next to the harbor; but if by chance you don't see the tents and tables, just follow your nose—the smell of fish is undeniable.

Along the length of the old city's "**pedestrian zone,**" you will see various historic buildings, municipal centers, and churches. Take note of any placards posted on the buildings stating the year of construction or any other historical note of interest—you may well be surprised by the city's diversity.

Rijeka's Center

Map of Trsat (COURTESY OF RIJEKA TOURIST BOARD)

1 – **Trsatski park** / Trsat Gardens
2 – **Crkva Gospe Trsatske i franjevački samostan** /
 Our Lady of Trsat Church and Franciscan Monastery
3 – **Hrvatska čitaonica na Trsatu** / Croatian Reading Room Trsat

4 – **Župna crkva sv. Jurja** / Parish Church of St. George
5 – **Trsatska gradina** / Trsat Castle
6 – **Dvorana mladosti** / Youth Sports Hall

After the tour of the old city, take a short walk uphill and find a good spot to take a panoramic picture of the city and have lunch overlooking the water—or even dinner as the sun sets. A special treat for you when you reach the top of the hill is Rijeka's famous **Trsat** (*ter-saht*), a dynamic complex featuring a castle, gardens, and more. It is a bit of a hike, but well worth the time. From the city center (harbor), move east until you reach **Titov trg** (*teatove terg*). From the trg, you proceed to **Stube Petra Kružića** (*stew-bah paztra crew-zheat-zah*) (also called the **Trsatske stube** [*ter-sat-skeh stew-bah*]) "Petar Kružić steps," up the hill to the **Crkva Gospe Trsatske i franjevački samostan** (*sirk-vah goss-pay ter-sat-skay e fran-yea-vach-key sahm-o-stahn*), "Our Lady of Trsat Church and Franciscan Monastery," on the right side. On the left, lies the **Hrvatska čitaonica na Trsatu** (*her-vaht-skah cheat-ah-own-eatsah nah ter-sah-two*), the "Croatian reading room trsat." Turn left toward the reading center and you come to the **Župna crkva sv. Jurija** (*zhupe-nah sirk-vah sve-toge your-ee-ah*), the "parish church of Saint George," and behind that, at the apex, you will reach the **castle**, where you can catch a glimpse of all of the other sites that lie within your reach.

Useful Web Sites

www.dalmatia.hr
www.kvarner.hr
www.rijeka.hr
www.ri-karneval.com.hr
www.summernet.hr
www.tz-rijeka.hr

Rijeka Highlights

Harbor
Pedestrian zone
Trsat
University of Rijeka

BIOGRAD NA MORU

Population: Approx. 5,000
Claim to Fame: Party Center

Biograd na moru (*bea-o-grahd nah more-oo*) is know for being one of the most popular tourist centers among Croats, due to its fairs, concerts, amusement parks, and other attractions, such as candy shops and clowns. Biograd itself is a quaint town, but the countryside around Biograd is not yet redeveloped for tourists. A quick tour of the area around Biograd will reveal a devastated and empty desert, devoid of any signs of life since the war in the 1990s, because the area suffered greatly from heavy attacks from both sides. A quick drive will tell a thousand tales, but be careful not to venture off the road.

Useful Web Sites

http://biograd.info
www.biogradnamoru.hr
www.val-tours.hr

ZADAR

Population: Approx. 72,000
Claim to Fame: The City Walls and Magnificent Churches

Some of the main highlights of the beautiful coastal city of **Zadar** (*zah-dahr*) include the city walls, the entire **harbor** area, and, of course, the **beach**. The city walls enclose much of the old city, which contains many ancient sites of interest. The great **market** next to the harbor is also fascinating. Like other markets in Croatia, this one is full of hustle and bustle, with everything from freshly caught fish and recently picked fruits to plastic toys made half a world away in China. If you like fish such as snapper, and are staying in a hotel or apartment with your own kitchen, get it here at the market and prepare it yourself, using some fresh lemon and other easy-to-find ingredients. Just ask the fish salesman for **zubatac** (*zoo-bah-tats*), "snapper." The market has so many practical goods that you can pack lightly for your trip and buy things

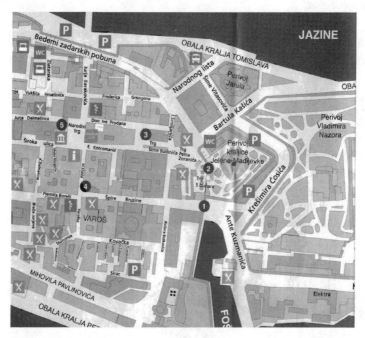

Zadar (COURTESY OF ZADAR TOURIST BOARD)

1 – **Kopnena vrata** / The Land Gate
2 – **Trg 5 Bunara** / The Five Wells Square
3 – **Crkva sv. Šime** / Church of Saint Simeon
4 – **Crkva i samostan sv. Mihovila** / Church and Monastery of Saint Michael
5 – **Gradska Straža** / The City Sentinel

Church in Zadar

such as flip-flops, swimwear, suntan lotion, and umbrellas at the harborside market—and it is always inexpensive!

One of the oldest Croatian cities, Zadar boasts almost three millennia of organized settlement. First settled by Illyrians, the city became a legal part of Rome in 59 BC. As a flourishing port city, Zadar remained important when the Roman Empire split into Eastern and Western halves; the city emerged as the capital of the Byzantine (Eastern Roman Empire) province of Dalmatia.

In the early Middle Ages, the rebirth of Italian city-states, especially Venice, brought a new presence to the Balkan Peninsula—including in Zadar. The city suffered during the Second Crusade because of its position on the coast; in 1202 the city was sacked by marauding crusaders on their way to the Holy Land. The entire incident led to condemnation from the reigning pope, but the damage was already done. Zadar underwent renovation but never fully recovered its formerly prosperous state. Handed back and forth between the Hungarians and various Italian states, the heavily fortified but economically damaged city of Zadar ended up first a part of France (Illyrian Provinces), then Austria in the early nineteenth century, and then in 1918, became a part of the new Yugoslavia. Zadar did not remain part

Typical seaside walls along the Dalmation Coast

of Yugoslavia for long, though, because in 1920 the city was transferred to Italy's control and only returned to Yugoslavia after World War II. The culture in Zadar reveals a rich history. As home to the first newspaper in the Croatian language—called the **Krajlevski Dalmatin** (*cry-lev-ski doll-mah-teen*), founded in 1806, Zadar boasts a long tradition of educational excellence. Near what is today St. Dominic's Church is an old stone building, adorned by a plaque, proclaiming this as the site of the first university on Croatian soil. It was founded in 1386 by Dominican monks, and although it is not quite as old as some other European universities such as Cambridge (1303), Heidelberg (1385), or Charles University in Prague (1348), the locals in Zadar are still proud of its long heritage.

If you enjoy visiting churches, Zadar will not disappoint you. With over thirty churches, including the biggest cathedral in Dalmatia, **St. Anastasia,** built during the twelfth and thirteenth centuries, Zadar is a rich area of religious history.

The city walls around the old town with the historic gates built in 1543— the **Kopnena vrata** (*cope-nay-nah vrah-tah*)—and 1573—the **Lučka vrata** (*looch-kah vrah-tah*)—are most impressive. Over the years men have tried to scale the high city walls without climbing equipment, but no one has ever succeeded because the walls are extremely smooth and slick. The perfect record of failure, however, does not stop diehards from trying—each summer starts a new round of attempts by rock climbers, and you might witness one of these.

Today, Zadar boasts some impressive architecture, although the buildings are devoid of any uniformity. Because of its location on the sea, Zadar has been easy prey over the centuries to invasions, and despite the good fortifications, many buildings have been ruined and rebuilt in different traditions. Arguably the most destructive period in recent history occurred during World War II, when the city was bombed and many buildings in the old town were left in rubble. The wars in former Yugoslavia during the 1990s left many scars in Zadar as well, but the damage was not longlasting. The city was shelled for a short time because it served as a center for resistance against the Serbian forces throughout the area. Secured by 1993 by the Croatian government, the city quickly underwent reconstruction and by the end of the decade was functioning again as a hub of tourist activity.

Be sure to stop by the **Tourist Office** at 5 Ilije Smiljanića (*ill-ee-yah smee-lee-yan-eatsa*) to pick up extra materials such as maps or local accommodation guides. A visit should include a short tour of the periphery to get a feel for the area and to see some of the outlying sites. A walk around the old city will only take about two hours without stops, but with breaks at the various sites, plan on spending the majority of a day taking in what Zadar has to offer. The hidden cobblestone streets lined with cafés, ice cream shops, and hidden restaurants serving up fresh fish and pasta dishes for lunch and dinner are more than worth the time spent.

Useful Web Sites

www.tzzadar.hr
www.zadar.hr
www.zadaronline.com

Split

Population: Approx. 250,000
Claim to Fame: Diocletian's Palace

Like other coastal cities in Dalmatia, Split has a long and tumultuous history. It is believed that a Greek colony settled in the area but fell victim to Roman expansion in the second or third centuries. The Roman emperor Diocletian (ruled from AD 284–305) ordered that a tremendous palace be built for him in what is today the old city center of Split. This area of the palace became the site for later settlements, serving as a ready-made fortified city-state with influence over the Adriatic and the coast.

Split came under the authority of the early Dalmatian duchy and Croatian kingdom but fell prey to Venetian naval prowess in 1420. Despite the Venetian presence, Split was able to secure for itself favorable commercial and

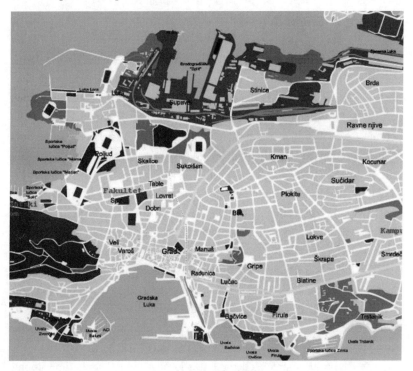

Old City of Split

The Riva in Split

political rights and prospered greatly as a result of the conquest. It was during this time that many important cultural advances were made in Split; the city rivals Dubrovnik in its importance in early Croatian literature and linguistics.

Like the other cities controlled by Venice, Split witnessed the brief period of Napoleonic rule and thereafter became an Austrian province. Split escaped annexation by Italy following World War I, and because important port cities like Zadar and Pula became tied to Italy, Split grew into a very important port city for the new Yugoslavia. Mussolini saw to it that during World War II Split become a part of Italy, but the Italian rule during this brief period left no imprint. Split returned to Yugoslavia in 1945 and has prospered as a major shipping and tourist center ever since.

The Split of today is a hub for Croatian economic and cultural life. As the second largest city in the country, Split has a large university and with it a thriving student community. The cafés in Split are famous, and a series of them dot the entire coastal area between the old city and the harbor. The most famous café street is located along the water next to the old city—this must be seen to be appreciated—and it is lovely to spend some time sipping a drink while watching hundreds if not thousands of people pass by.

Emperor Diocletian's Palace

The heart of the old city lies behind this café street, and walking around will reveal numerous delights, such as **Diocletian's Palace** and dozens of small museums and shops that boast a unique history in their own right. One of the treasures of the palace is what archaeologists uncovered during a renovation procedure; during Roman times and even shortly thereafter, the residents of the palace disposed of their garbage, including broken pots, miscellaneous handicrafts, and much more, in the basement of the palace, which was later covered over with marble and left unnoticed for centuries. Today, an interesting exhibition displays some of these pieces as part of a broader glimpse into life long ago. The market also lies close to the old city and serves to bind the old city with the new.

Finding a good place to eat in Split is simple, and finding accommodations is just as easy. The only catch is that the accommodations might not be within walking distance—or rather, the less expensive accommodations might not be within walking distance of the center. The city bus system in Split is good, the stops are clearly marked on the streets, and maps of the bus routes are easy to obtain. Generally speaking, if you need to take a bus to reach the old city and all it has to offer, a bus ride with the

Split's main pedestrian zone

local city dwellers and tourists alike will prove a "cultural" experience in its own right.

One of the things to keep in mind as you walk around Split is that, as in Zadar, you will observe a hodgepodge of architectural designs throughout the city. This is in part the result of warfare over the centuries, but you can see a fairly consistent Italian note throughout the city.

Getting There

The bus station is situated at **Obala Kneza Domagoja** 12 (*o-bah-lah kah-nez-ah dough-mah-goy-ah*) in the city center on the east side of Diocletian's Palace, the landmark that forms the heart of Split. A short walk away is the harbor (see www.portsplit.com for more) and the railway station (at **Domagojeva obala** 9 [*dough-mah-goy-ehva*]), tel.: 021/338-525 and 060/333-444). The excellent connections in and out of the city provide plenty of options in planning a trip. Bus travel is probably the most popular means of transportation in Croatia, especially among locals, but travel by passenger ferry is also very fashionable and affords a pleasant way to tour the Dalmatian coast. During the high season, passenger ships of all sizes frequently leave for Dubrovnik, Rijeka, and the multitude of small islands and cities all over

Croatia. The boats are not the fastest mode of transportation—but they are not the slowest either, and the appeal of catching the sunset from the top deck of a ferry or seeing a small island or rock formation up close from a boat while sharing a glass of wine with your loved one or family is unbeatable.

Useful Web Sites

Central Bus Station: www.ak-split.hr
www.split.hr
www.split.info
www.visitsplit.com

Split Highlights

Art Gallery (www.galum.hr)
Croatian Archeological Museum (www.mhas-split.hr)
Croatian National Theater Split (www.hnk-split.hr)
Museum of Split (www.mgst.net)
The Split Film Festival (www.splitfilmfestival.hr)
The Split Youth City Theater (www.gkm.hr)

TROGIR

Population: 8,500
Claim to Fame: The Museum City

Trogir (*trow-gear*) is situated on a small island that is connected to Croatia's mainland and the neighboring island of Čiovo (*chee-o-vow*) by bridges. Trogir lies incredibly close to Split; so close that some refer to it as Split's little sibling. A haven for tourists, the best of Trogir can be taken in during a day-long walk through the large open-air museum, which displays some beautiful examples of the architectural skills of the town's initial Greco-Roman colonizers. The United Nations Scientific, Cultural, and Education Organization (UNESCO) named this jewel of ancient architecture as a World Heritage Site in 1997 to establish a permanent monument to the classical style and overwhelming cultural wealth that Trogir has to offer.

For a helpful city map, visit the Trogir tourist information office on the main square—**Trg Ivana Pavla II** (*terg ee-vahn-ah pave-lah drew-ge*)—or just walk along the east coast of Trogir and you will pass both the cathedral and the mayor's office until you reach the **Church of St. Nicolas** and the monastery that hosts one of the two remaining reliefs of Kairos dating back to the third century before Christ. Continue walking to the west side to the fortress of **Kamerlengo**, which is an enormous naval base that was built by the Venetians during the thirteenth, fourteenth, and fifteenth centuries. Nowadays, without a military purpose, the fortress fights for culture by serving as an open-air cinema and as host to many special cultural events and festivals.

As a symbol of their power in the area, the Venetians erected statues of lions all over Dalmatia, and any cursory glance around the towns and villages along the coast will remind one of this Italian influence. One thing that sets Trogir apart, however, is that during the rise of fascism in Italy and its expansionistic rhetoric, the inhabitants of Trogir destroyed almost all of the statues in protest on the night of January 1, 1932.

Useful Web Sites

www.trogir.org
www.trogir-ciovo.info
www.trogir-online.com

DUBROVNIK

Population: Approx. 56,000
Claim to Fame: The Historical City on the Peninsula

The Jewel of the Adriatic

What made the "Jewel of the Adriatic" so famous? **Dubrovnik** (*dew-brove-nick*) boasts a rich beauty and a colorful and influential history. As a bridge between historic tribal groups, Dubrovnik emerged as a city of major importance during the twelfth century with the construction of the main plaza and later of fortifications and harbors. Under the jurisdiction of the

View of Dubrovnik

Byzantine Empire, Dubrovnik prospered from trade with the Near East and competed with the emerging Italian city-states for power in the Adriatic and the Eastern Mediterranean. From 1205 to 1358 though, Dubrovnik was controlled by Venice, only to be traded off to the Croatian-Hungarian kingdom instead of gaining independence. But clever statesmen in Dubrovnik whittled away at this overlordship and achieved free status for Dubrovnik. It is at this point that Dubrovnik was referred to as the Republic of Ragusa. This free status peaked in the fifteenth and sixteenth centuries, when the city competed vigorously with Venice; and like Venice, it was ruled by aristocratic elites and continued to prosper as long as the Mediterranean remained the major source of wealth for Europe. Naturally, this changed with the discovery of the New World and the subsequent shift to oceangoing naval power. An earthquake in 1667 also destroyed much of the city, and today's baroque-style architecture in Dubrovnik was built during the city's reconstruction.

Dubrovnik managed to remain free from outside control until 1806, when Napoleonic forces began aggressive actions in the area, and by 1808, the city formed a part of the Illyrian Provinces. After 1815, Austria took over the city and it remained under Austrian control until the end of World War I.

During these periods as a free state and under Austrian rule, Dubrovnik flowered as the cultural capital of Croatia. With numerous famous poets, writers, painters, and sculptors, Dubrovnik society made a large imprint on Croatian culture. Two of the most famous residents include literary figure Ivan Gundulić and physicist Ruder Bošković (1717–1787). As a center for trade, the city also served as a hub for cultural exchange and benefited from progress made in neighboring cities and faraway lands alike.

As was the case for most of the Croatian coast, the city changed hands several times during the first half of the twentieth century as a result of the struggle between Italy and Yugoslavia for the Adriatic seaports. Dubrovnik, of course, became a formal part of Croatia as part of Tito's Yugoslav state. But when Tito's state began to fall apart violently in the early 1990s, the most dramatic struggle over the city of Dubrovnik caught the attention of the world as a result of shelling by the Yugoslav navy and by an army

Dubrovnik's old town

artillery unit. Intermittently under fire until the summer of 1992, much of the city, including historic buildings and especially the fragile rooftops, suffered some damage. Fortunately, though, the United Nations teamed up with the government of Croatia to restore the city, and today's Dubrovnik is indeed a jewel to be enjoyed.

What do you do first to get the most from Dubrovnik? The old city is so small that it is possible to do a lot in a short amount of time, but because there is so much to see and do, two or three weeks could easily be taken up in various activities.

The first order of business should be to go into the old city through the labyrinth of streets, paths, and staircases to experience the architecture, the handicraft shops, the restaurants, and the crowds of people having a coffee in one of the innumerable outdoor cafés. Dubrovnik is probably one of the

Downtown Dubrovnik

best examples of how the past and present combine. If you want ruins and a guide telling you what this or that building was used for, you can of course find that in Dubrovnik. Yet Dubrovnik is in part famous for its everyday simplicity, which embraces history and culture in a much more refined manner than is the case for Venice or Rome. While the museums and churches must be seen, it is just as important to discover a small, hidden schoolyard where children are playing, or a courtyard where locals are gossiping or arguing sports over a beer.

Any of the tourist books published by the city will list and describe the spots of interest, in addition to many helpful business advertisements that may lead you to a very useful Internet café or popular casino. Most important, though, is the listing of upcoming events in the city that is found in the regularly published tourist guide. Featuring countless musical engagements of all varieties, artistic shows, and theatrical performances, this list will ensure against boredom. The local university in Dubrovnik—itself an article of historical importance—also sponsors numerous courses or programs of interest to academics and tourists alike, running the gamut from conferences to language courses.

A must in Dubrovnik is taking a **walk along the city walls** to view the panorama of the beach below and the city that has sprawled out from this ancient settlement. Be sure to look out for historic pieces of artillery and

Hidden Café outside the walls of Dubrovnik

Map of the old city of Dubrovnik (Courtesy of Dubrovnik Tourist Board)

Legend:

Express sightseeing tour — 30 min
North sightseeing tour — 1 h
South sightseeing tour — 2 h
Full sightseeing tour — 3,5 h

Brza turistička ruta
Sjeverna turistička ruta
Južna turistička ruta
Cjelokupna turistička ruta

* Approx. time of the tour. For individual attractions time is not included!
* Približno trajanje rute! Vrijeme potrebno za posjetu atrakcijama nije uključeno!

1. Pile Gate — Gradska vrata Pile
2. Entrance to the City Walls — Ulaz u gradske zidine
3. Church of St Saviour — Crkva sv. Spasa
4. Big Onofrio's Fountain — Velika Onofrijeva fontana
5. Franciscan Monastery-Museum — Franjevački samostan-muzej
6. Stradun-Placa — Stradun-Placa
7. Orlando's Column — Orlandov stup
8. Sponza Palace-Historic Archives — Sponza-Povijesni arhiv
9. Bell tower and bell lounge — Gradski zvonik i zvonara
10. Small Onofrio's Fountain — Mala Onofrijeva fontana
11. St Blaise Church — Crkva sv. Vlaha
12. City theatre Marin Držić Theatre — Gradsko kazalište Marina Držića
13. Rector's Palace — Knežev dvor

14. Old Port — Gradska luka
15. Cathedral-Treasury — Katedrala - riznica
16. Gundulić's Square — Gundulićeva poljana
17. St Catherine Convent — Samostan sv. Katarine
18. Ethnographic Museum Rupe — Etnografski muzej Rupe
19. Home of Marin Držić — Dom Marina Držića
20. Homeland war exhibition — Izložba Domovinskog rata
21. Synagogue-Museum — Sinagoga-muzej
22. St Nicholas Church — Crkva sv. Nikole
23. St Sebastian Church — Crkva sv. Sebastijana
24. Church and Confraternity Rosario — Crkva i bratovština Rozario
25. Dominican Monastery-Museum — Dominikanski samostan-muzej
26. City wall entrance — Ulaz na gradske zidine
27. St John Fort — Tvrđava sv. Ivana
28. Maritime Museum — Pomorski muzej
29. Aquarium — Akvarium
30. Fort Bokar — Tvrđava Bokar
31. Fort Minčeta — Tvrđava Minčeta
32. IUC & MGHS — IUC & MGHS
33. Fort Lovrijenac — Tvrđava Lovrijenac
34. Former Convent of St Claire — Bivši samostan sv. Klare
35. Sigurata Church — Crkva Sigurata
36. Prijeko street — Prijeko
37. Serbian Orthodox Church and Museum of Icons — Srpska pravoslavna crkva i muzej ikona
38. Mosque (Masjed) — Džamija
39. Fort Revelin — Tvrđava Revelin
40. Ploče Gate — Vrata od Ploča
41. Lazarettos (Quarantine) — Lazareti
42. Church of Annunciation and of St Luke — Crkva Navještenja i sv. Luke
43. North city entrance (Buža) — Crkva Navještenja i sv. Luke (Buža)
44. St Ignatius Church — Crkva Sv. Ignacija

Dubrovnik tourist board info offices
Info uredi
Turistička zajednica grada Dubrovnika

PILE, Branitelja Dubrovnika 7, Tel: ++385(0)20 427 591, 426 253

various fortification redoubts. The next must-see is **St. Blaise Church**, which stands at the end of the long pedestrian walkway in the old city opposite the **Gradska kavana** (*grahd-skah kah-vah-nah*), the "city coffee house," and a shopping center complete with movie theater. Walk around St. Blaise Church as if you were going to enter the church from the rear. Head in this direction and you will find the cathedral surrounded by lovely marble and stone steps. Continue up the steps and explore the small streets that lead to the city walls. Walk on these inside streets up to two small doorways leading through the city walls. One of these doors leads to a small rocky beach, while the other goes to another rocky beach, home to the famous **Café**. The views from these two hidden spots are great—especially for catching a sunset or observing Lokrum Island, only a few hundred yards away.

Lokrum Island is a small hideaway that is well worth a short visit. From the port in the old city—called **Ploče** (*plough-che*)—there are frequent trips back and forth all day long. The best thing to do is to take a late morning ride and have a picnic lunch on one of the beaches or hilltops overlooking Dubrovnik. The walkways on the island are clean and well kept and lead to a series of interesting spots. During the high season a few cafés are open, as well as some restaurants, so there is no problem if you forget to bring a water bottle or some snacks.

Back on the mainland, venture up to the **top of the mountain** overlooking Dubrovnik. You cannot miss this icon—there is an abandoned, modern-day **fortress** and a giant **cross** that was also built after the last war, both to show the Catholic identity of the city's inhabitants and as a safeguard against evil. While a walk from the old city up the mountain might seem daunting, it only takes about forty-five minutes, and the paths are well marked. Just keep going uphill. At the top there is a beautiful panorama stretching for miles in all directions. The view from here is absolutely spectacular and is a prize for any photographer, amateur and professional alike.

The many hotels, casinos, and other tourist centers throughout the city—old and new—offer a tremendous variety of things to do. From scuba diving, canoeing, and sailing to horseback riding, jeep tours, and daily excursions to nearby islands such as Mljet, there is aways something fun and exciting to do. Many of the larger hotels, museums, and outings are family friendly, with activities not aimed solely at adults.

Dalmatian village harbor

St. Mark's Cathedral in Zagreb

(*Top/left*) Quiet beach

(*Left*) Waterside church

(*Top/right*) Rest and relaxation on a Croatian beach

(*Bottom/right*) Zagreb's Art Pavilion

(*left*) Stone stairway in Dubrovnik

(*right*) Old Town Rovinj

View of
Dubrovnik
Harbor

(left) Plitvice
waterfalls

(top) Castle in
Hrvatsko Zagorje
Region

(bottom)
Stunning nature
of Croatian
landscape

The tranquil
coastline of
Croatia

Greater Dubrovnik (Courtesy of Dubrovnik Tourist Board)

Getting There

Croats have made it very easy for you to visit Dubrovnik, their most highly prized city. In addition to the excellent air connections from Zagreb, many more cities such as Frankfurt now offer direct and convenient flights to Dubrovnik. The airport is located in nearby **Cavtat**, a small tourist destination in its own right, with a small beach and quaint old town. A taxi ride to the center of Dubrovnik can prove expensive, but fortunately, just like in Zagreb, Croatia Airlines operates a shuttle bus to two points in Dubrovnik: the old city gates, called **Pile** (*pea-lay*) and the main bus station in **Lapad** (*lah-pahd*). From the main station in Lapad you can catch any local bus or hail a taxi to your hotel. The timetables are posted for the buses at Lapad and are clear enough to be understood without knowledge of Croatian. When staying in or near the old city, getting out at Pile is the best option. The cost for the Croatian Airlines bus is a few kuna more expensive than in Zagreb, but it is clean, comfortable, fast, punctual, and reliable. From the airport, go outside and you will either see one of the buses or one of the several signs listing the time schedule and price. The buses should run every half hour, but double-check the airport Web site before leaving (www.airport-dubrovnik.hr).

A second way to reach Dubrovnik is by boat. The harbor in Dubrovnik is spacious and caters to individuals with their private crafts and to a host of passenger ferries. Increasingly, Mediterranean cruise ships make port in Dubrovnik as part of their tour schedule. The harbor is located near the bus station at Lapad, but since it is long and narrow it stretches for several hundred yards away from the bus station. The Jadrolinija ferry company operates a small branch office, which is clearly marked with the schedule for passenger ferry service. A very good way to end your time in Dubrovnik is to sail away on one of these ferries to continue your vacation farther up the coast in a city such as Split.

The final major mode of transportation in and out of Dubrovnik is the bus. As previously stated, bus service in Croatia is very good, and so are the connections to Dubrovnik. Bear in mind that between renting a car in Zagreb or taking the bus, the latter may be faster because the buses have their own lanes at the border, and if the trip requires a ferry, the buses have priority. And do not forget that American citizens and citizens of the European Union (EU) do not need a visa for transit through Bosnia-Herzegovina (a small section of land, centered in the city of Neum is part of Bosnia, and the Croatian highway must pass through it). If traveling with someone who might need a visa for Bosnia, check in advance with the nearest Bosnian embassy (check for American and EU citizens as well, just to be sure). In case a visa issue arises, the ferry from Split is a great alternative to ground transport. With multiple connections from cities throughout Croatia, the Balkans, and many places in Europe (there is a bus from Frankfurt, but such a journey may take some twenty-four hours) you can always arrive or leave via bus. From Dubrovnik, bus travel also affords the luxury of taking a trip to Bosnia-Herzegovina—you can reach either Međugorje, the famous Catholic retreat where the Virgin Mary appeared; Mostar, with its famous bridge built by the Ottoman Turks (included on the UNESCO World Heritage list); or Sarajevo, with its spectacular Turkish market, offering the world's best **ćevapi** (*che-vah-pee*) and **burek** (*boo-reck*) (a mixed-meat sausage with spices and pita bread, and a baked meat or cheese-filled pastry, respectively). You can also make the short trip to Montenegro, also on the Dalmatian coast, including the renowned Bay of Kotor. For all of the connections—both national and international—check the Web site at www.libertasdubrovnik.hr for more information.

Useful Web Sites

http://en.dubrovnatic.net
www.dubrovnik4u.com
www.dubrovnikapartments-laptalo.com.hr
www.dubrovnik-area.com
www.dubrovnik-online.com
www.dubrovnikphotos.com
www.dubrovnikprivatetours.com
www.dubrovnik-travel.com
www.tzdubrovnik.hr
www.visitdubrovnik.hr

CHAPTER 8

THE ISLANDS

Croatia has 1,185 islands, of which 47 are inhabited. While the coast is spectacular and not to be missed, the islands make a visit to Croatia really special. No other country in Europe offers the same experience. Ideally, your vacation would include a visit to several islands, since each has its own special qualities—**Hvar** is reputed to have the most sunlight of any island, while **Korčula** claims the famous Marco Polo, and **Pag** is home to the famous Croatian goat cheese, **paški sir** (*pash-key sear*).

The islands are all connected by an excellent transportation network primarily run by Jadrolinija (see Web site at www.jadrolinija.com). Travel to and from the various islands is easy and relatively inexpensive. Check out Chapter

Hvar marina

4, pages 45–46, on ferry transportation. In addition, on the most popular islands private tour companies offer excursions to nearby hideaways. Usually lasting one day, these excursions typically include a picnic lunch (generally a choice of meat or fish, though increasingly catering to vegetarian needs) and allow for free time on the various islands to visit quaint little villages or isolated beaches.

The tourist agencies along the Dalmatian coast and islands offer advanced sources of information for excursions and also up-to-date information for arriving tourists. The agencies exist in Croatia similar to a tourist office or bureau in the United States. This is different from the United States, where a tourist agency is not designed to cater to tourists on the spot. When planning a trip to any island, do a quick online search of the island and click on some of the links. Get a sense for what is being offered online, and then make a few contacts.

CRES AND LOŠINJ

Population: Approx. 14,000
Claim to Fame: Flora and Fauna

Cres (*sres*) in the north and Lošinj (*low-sheen*) in the south are islands divided only by a small channel in the village of Osor, but are connected by a moving bridge. The two islands have quite diverse flora and fauna and therefore offer great potential for day-long hikes or simply for after-dinner walks.

Cres is the main city on the island of Cres and features a large marina in a beautiful bay. The picturesque town is directly on the water, which makes it a great spot to just sit and relax with an ice cream or a cold drink. The town market is also home to a great variety of fresh fish and fruits, so if you are camping or have a kitchen in an apartment, you can cook a delightful meal. In the upper northern part of the island enjoy the large panorama of **Beli** (*belly*) and the impressive, huge freshwater lake called **Vransko jezero** (*vrahn-skoe ye-sehr-oh*), which supplies both islands with fresh water. The lake can be viewed only from a distance, since to protect the purity of the water people are prohibited by the government from going in or near the water. Another great aspect of Cres is the fine panorama from **Ustrine** (*oos-tree-nah*) and there is also a nudist camp and beach at **Punta križa** (*poon-tah kree-zhah*).

The small town of **Osor** is known for its beautiful church, which holds regular concerts, and a host of small art galleries. Although tiny, it is worth a visit during a stay on either Cres or Lošinj.

Lošinj is a diver's paradise and has three major townships: **Nerezine, Mali Lošinj,** and **Veli Lošinj.** Nerezine (*nay-ray-zee-nay*) is equipped with an attractive marina and is the nearest town to Cres with good shopping facilities. Mali Lošinj (*mah-lee low-sheen*, which means "Small Lošinj") is in fact bigger than Veli Lošinj (*vell-ee low-sheen*, which means "Big Lošinj") and is a great place for enjoying a café atmosphere, vibrant nightlife, and shopping. In contrast, Veli Lošinj is a sleepy cove perfect for the easygoing tourist seeking peace and tranquility.

From either Mali Lošinj or Veli Lošinj you can book one-day tours to the car-free islands of **Susak** (*sue-sak*) or **Unije** (*oo-knee-yay*) and experience a bit of variety to island life.

Useful Web Sites

www.island-cres.net
www.island-losinj.com
www.losinj-val.com

Mali Lošinj from the water

KRK

Population: Approx. 18,000
Claim to Fame: Bašćanska ploča

Krk (*kirk*) is the most densely populated Adriatic island and ties with the neighboring island of Cres as the largest. Krk lies near to the large industrial and tourist city of Rijeka, so close in fact that you can easily make out some of Rijeka's buildings from various points on Krk. In 1980, the Yugoslav authorities completed a bridge connecting Krk with the mainland. One of the longest concrete bridges in the world—spanning over 4,200 feet—the bridge has facilitated the development of a vibrant tourist industry. Located a few hours drive from northern Italy, southern Germany, Austria, and Slovenia, Krk has successfully expanded a convenient and modern transportation network catering to foreign tourists. Bus connections from all points in Croatia are excellent, as are ferries, including car ferries that connect with neighboring islands such as Cres (and Lošinj).

Krk has an airport, located at the north end of the island, and many scattered villages and towns, most of them equipped with everything from restaurants and lazy cafés to bus stations and large hotels. With almost any recreational activity available on Krk, you are sure to find a place to scuba dive, snorkel, water ski, fish, or swim. The numerous beaches are well appointed with services such as cafés, small eateries specializing in small fish (**ribice** *rib-ee-tse*)—for more see Chapter 14). If you drive to the island from another point in Croatia, you should only need approximately two to two and a half hours from Zagreb, even during high season when the highways are congested. The drive from Zagreb is quite scenic, and is a trip in and of itself. Much of the countryside to the west of Croatia's capital presents a rural alpine landscape similar to Austria or southern Germany. The lush forests and mountains slowly change into a rocky coastline marked by scrub brush. On the island of Krk itself, the variety of vegetation increases and you can even find a few forests.

The primary center of activity on Krk is the main city of **Krk**, home to the **marina** and commercial **port, historic ruins,** mostly dating from the fifteenth century, and the most diverse tourist services. If you have access to a

Tower of the court of law in Krk

car or even a bicycle, don't miss the opportunity to visit some of the smaller towns and scattered villages. With churches dating back hundreds of years, bell towers, libraries, fossil collections, and museums featuring Croatia's first written script—Glagolitic—you are sure to enjoy a diverse visit to Krk.

Useful Web Sites

www.aurea-krk.hr
www.isola-di-krk.net/croatia
www.istria.info/en/krk/krk.php
www.krk.hr
www.krkholiday.com
www.krkinfo.com

Rab

Population: Approx. 9,500
Claim to Fame: Haven for Nudists

Closely connected to the island of Krk throughout history—and today by frequent ferry connections as well—the island of **Rab** (*rahb*) serves as an oasis for vacationers seeking **wellness resorts** as well as nudists seeking comfortable places to sunbathe and swim.

The history of Rab is typical for the Croatian coast: Illyrian settlements followed by Roman rule, then a mix of Croatian, Hungarian, Italian, and Austrian control. Some of the medieval buildings still remain, including private buildings as well as churches.

Useful Web Sites

www.croatia-islandrab.com
www.croatia-rab.com
www.kristofor.hr
www.otokrab.hr (offering a huge list of accommodations)

Pag

Population: Approx. 5,000
Claim to Fame: Paški sir

Another of the central Dalmatian islands, **Pag** (*pahg*) has both a rich and conflict-ridden history. Located close to Zadar and at a key point between Venice and the open waters of the Mediterranean, Pag has for centuries suffered as a result of the quarrels of other states. Wars between Balkan nobles, Venetian shipping magnates, and Ottoman treasure seekers meant that the inhabitants of the island frequently rebuilt and moved their residences and towns. The riches of the island, however, made it worthwhile to stay there. Currently responsible for over two-thirds of Croatia's total salt production, the island's rich salt resources over the centuries made many of the residents of Pag wealthy.

Handmade lace also ranks high on the list of valued items from Pag. Although this is not the only Dalmatian island famous for lace, it does produce some of the most highly prized examples. The island is far better known as a preserve for sheep and, as a result of this important and large industry, a widely known and sought-after cheese—**paški sir** (*pash-key sear*), "cheese from Pag." The unique taste of this cheese comes from the rare blend of aromatic herbs and grasses that the sheep feed on.

Rocks dominate the island's landscape and thus provide a diverse experience for the visitor. Along the water, the rocks give a swimmer a private escape from busy beaches while they give a hiker a sense of splended barrenness despite the many thousands of sheep that thrive on the rocky hills.

Tourist services are well established on Pag, but don't expect large hotels with multiple restaurants and casinos. The primary means of accommodation is private houses. When going to Pag—as is the case for other islands where you can rent a private apartment—check with a local tourist agency for price and availability.

Useful Web Sites

www.apartmani-simuni.com
www.novalja.com
www.novalja-pag.net/mandre/gligora
www.pag-tourism.hr

VIR

Population: Approx. 1,600
Claim to Fame: Weekend retreat for citizens of Zadar

Vir (*veer*) offers visitors pleasant **beaches** and great sites for **camping**—complete with pine trees—but there are two drawbacks: thousands of construction sites and, especially on the weekends, masses of people arriving from Zadar via the bridge to the mainland. Known by the locals as an island of contrasts, Vir is home to quaint private apartments and old-style dwellings as well as modern mansions and piers for visiting yacht owners. With excellent deep-sea diving opportunities as well as boat rental services, the island is a nautical gem.

Useful Web Site

www.otok-vir.info

Ugljan and Pašman

Population: Approx. 1,000
Claim to Fame: Roman ruins

Ugljan (*oo-glee-an*) is a small getaway close to the major tourist center of Zadar. With seven villages in addition to the town of Ugljan, visitors can expect to see a lot during their stay on the island. Famous for its quality olive oil and ancient **Roman ruins,** the island is a relaxing retreat from the hustle and bustle of Zadar. The journey from Zadar is quick, owing to the close proximity of the island to the mainland. In addition, the small island of **Pašman** (*pash-man*) is connected to Ugljan by a bridge and as a result is accessible by foot, bike, or car.

Because of the strong Roman presence on the island and the vast number of surviving relics, a trip to the beach can be supplemented by a tour of a castle or ancient Roman villa.

Useful Web Sites

www.islandpasman.com
www.ugljan.hr
www.ugljan-pasman.com

Kornati

Claim to Fame: National Park

For more on the national park in **Kornati** (*core-nah-tea*), see Chapter 9, page 160.

Useful Web Site

www.kornati.hr

Brač

Population: Approx. 14,000
Claim to Fame: Marble used for the White House

Brač (*brach*) is the third largest Croatian island and has the highest mountain peak (**Vitus' Mountain**) of any Croatian island, reaching a height of 778 meters (almost 2,400 feet). With a diverse natural environment created by wind patterns and radical differences in elevation, the island's inhabitants have historically been involved in many different occupations. While fishing is a guaranteed source of livelihood for residents, the island's vineyards and olive groves account for much of the agricultural production. The results are excellent local wines and treats such as bread dipped in locally produced olive oil.

Croats on the island won't let you forget that it was marble from quarries on Brač that helped construct the White House in Washington, D.C. Brač marble, which in centuries past was always prized by political elites, today houses the contemporary world's most powerful leader. The Roman emperor Diocletian's palace in Split was also built using marble from the island of Brač.

While the main points of historical interest lie within the islands' towns and in the changing architectural styles that range over the centuries from Greco-Roman to Renaissance, a major tourist attraction is the famous **Zlatni rat beach** (*zhlat-knee raht*), renowned as one of the best in Croatia. Because Brač has limited water supplies, the vegetation is not as lush as that of other islands, but the rocky beaches have their own charm. Thousands upon thousands return to Brač year after year because of the great scuba diving, the beautiful coastline, and the excellent transportation connections. With flights from Zagreb and regular ferry service from all major points along the Croatian seaside, Brač is a great getaway.

Brač beach

Useful Web Sites

http://otok-brac.info
www.bracinfo.com
www.islandbrac.com
www.island-of-brac.info
www.welcome-to-croatia.com

HVAR

Population: Approx. 12,000
Claim to Fame: Sunniest spot in Europe and the Lavender Island

The island of **Hvar** (*quar*) is one of the most beautiful places in all of Dalmatia and many a visitor—foreign and domestic alike—has fallen in love with this sun-drenched island. Mankind took a liking to the island early on; indeed, some anthropologists believe that Hvar has some of the oldest human settlements in the Adriatic. Another important "first" for Hvar is that it was home to one of the first public theaters in Europe outside of Italy, which opened its doors in 1612.

Some of the important writers to have resided in this center of Croatian culture include Petar Hektorović and Hanibal Lučić. The residents of Hvar survive on tourism and fishing in addition to the arts. While boatbuilding was important in earlier centuries—as was the cultivation of certain plants such as lavender—Hvar has become known to all as the sunniest place in Europe, with an average of 2,715 sunlight hours (113 days) per year!

All of that sunshine makes a good recipe for fine wine, and Hvar wine is reknowned for its great taste. While visiting, be sure to walk around the towns and villages and keep your eye open for a winery. Chances are that you can walk in and sample some wine direct from the source!

One popular belief associated with the island's sunny climate is faith in the healthy effects of sunlight. A so-called Hygienic Society was founded in 1868 on Hvar, and a little over two decades later, a health spa opened for business. While the sun might improve your health, you are certainly guaranteed to have a good time on Hvar and more and more people agree: the *New York Times* has ranked Hvar one of the best travel destinations!

Typical Adriatic house

Useful Web Sites

http://w3.mrki.info/hvar
www.hvar.hr
www.hvarinfo.com
www.hvar-travel.com
www.island-hvar.info
www.sucuraj.com
www.sucuraj-hvar.com
www.sunnyhvar.com
www.tzhvar.hr/hr

KORČULA

Population: Approx. 16,000
Claim to Fame: Marco Polo's birthplace

Lying in the central Dalmatian region, the island of **Korčula** (*core-chew-lah*) is one of the larger Croatian islands and offers a typical Mediterranean climate. It is also known as the birthplace of Marco Polo. You are sure to find a lot of paraphernalia regarding Marco Polo. His official birthplace is slated to become a museum and don't be surprised to find souvenirs and even food dishes named after him (for example, Marco Polo Salad). Like most of the islands, the dominant attraction is the old town—in this case the town of Korčula, which features a rich variety of sights and distractions for visitors. With art galleries, museums, ancient monuments, and special events going on all summer long, something of interest is always taking place. Distinctive to Korčula is the historic Mediterranean folk dance, the **Moreška** ("sword dance"). The old city's major attractions include **St. Mark's Cathedral** (construction began in 1301) and the **palaces** of the Venetian governors.

With a history dating back to prehistoric times, the island was a part of Greece and Rome. More recently, however, its fate was tied to Venice and Austria-Hungary, and only in the last half century with Croatia. The variety of rulers over the island in part resulted from the island's strategic position at the point of entry of the Neretva River into the Adriatic. The Neretva is

Typical Croatian church

a primary river flowing out of Bosnia-Herzegovina and from the culturally rich city of Mostar.

A stay on the island of more than a day or two may provide time to explore the other places outside of the main town. A short bus ride in any direction will end up in any number of small villages, each offering something special such as a sand beach, a hidden winery, a medieval church, or historic ruins. You can't get lost, so feel free to venture out and explore—even on foot, but be sure to take plenty to drink if the sun is out, particularly while walking during the afternoon hours.

Useful Web Sites

www.apartment-korcula.com
www.island-korcula.info
www.korcula.ca
www.korcula.com

www.korcula.info
www.korcula.net
www.korcula-croatia.com
www.korculainfo.com
www.korcula-tours.com
www.mediterano.hr

MLJET

Population: Approx. 1,100
Claim to Fame: Island monastery

Mljet (*mlee-ett*) is a quaint little island only a short boat ride from Dubrovnik; it can be a stop on a longer ferry boat trip along the coast (for example, from Split to Dubrovnik). The island has several hidden treasures and many great opportunities for walks and rides. There are a few small villages on the island connected by good but narrow roads. From the harbor stop, you can walk up the street and there is at least one car rental agency offering small, 1960–70s-era Fiat convertibles or comparable little vehicles suitable for a short island

Mljet's Island Monastery

tour. A car is rather cheap, either by the day or for longer periods of time, and is quite fun. All the cars on Mljet—as with most of Croatia—are equipped with manual transmission, so for those who do not know how to drive a stick shift, a few quick lessons at home before renting something in Croatia would be in order.

In addition to an affordable car rental, there are plenty of bicycles or mopeds for rent in the vicinity of the harbor. There are many interesting things to see on Mljet, especially if you have any kind of transportation. There are only a few roads, so it is impossible to get lost—simply drive and when you feel like stopping, do so and enjoy!

You have to pass through a few villages from the harbor before reaching the major tourist centers of Mljet. Moving forward across the island, you will come to an attractive little settlement next to a small lake with lush vegetation. This example is not unique to Mljet; the variety of vegetation distinguishes Mljet from other areas in the Adriatic coast because, generally speaking, the heat and constant sunshine typical of the seaside usually only allow for scrub brush and a few tenacious trees. In contrast, though, Mljet offers a great variety of flora and fauna, and is always a few degrees cooler than nearby Dubrovnik. From this area near the lake you can see and easily reach the **island monastery**. Located on a small island in the middle of a saltwater inlet fed by the Adriatic, the monastery is open for tourists and should not be missed. First, however, continue driving to the other side of the monastery and follow the road until the end. You will emerge on a rocky beach facing the sea adorned with a small, concrete cross. From this isolated spot, the sharp contrasts between the mighty water current of the Adriatic and the calmer water that flows past to the very heart of the island and the monastery are clearly visible.

Following the roads back past the monastery is another part of the island with a small village equipped to handle tourist needs—food and drink! The few small restaurants are satisfactory and most are part of larger hotels, but all offer a good respite after a day of sightseeing on the island. Take your time on Mljet, because beyond each turn in the road or bend in the footpath, you will find something different and exciting.

Useful Web Sites

www.dubrovnikcity.com/guided/tours/mljettour.htm
www.dubrovnik-guide.net/mljet.htm
www.island-mljet.com
www.korcula.ws/futuratours/mljet1.asp
www.korcula-croatia.com/mljet.htm
www.korculainfo.com/mljet/map/map-mljet.htm
www.mljet.hr
www.mljettravel.com
www.np-mljet.hr
www.otokmljet.com

CHAPTER 9

ACTIVE PURSUITS

For those seeking an active vacation, Croatia offers virtually limitless possibilities all year round. During the summer, you can divide your time between music festivals and special art shows in cities such as Zagreb, and sailing, scuba diving, hiking, and catching up on your tan along the coast. In the winter months, you can take advantage of the ski slopes near Zagreb and end the day with a glass of warm wine on the main square.

NATIONAL PARKS

Before taking a deeper look at the specific outdoor activities, we want to emphasize the beauty of some of Croatia's national parks.

Plitvička jezera

First among these parks is **Plitvice**—or **Plitvička jezera** (*plit-vich-kah yeah-zer-ah*)—located about forty-five minutes from the city of Karlovac. Open year round, Plitvice nonetheless is more active during the peak season (April–October). At this time it is easy to take advantage of all the amenities located in the park, including the minibus, the boat ride, numerous hotels and restaurants, and of course, the endless hiking possibilities. If your trip to Croatia occurs in the wintertime, though, that has its charms as well. The authors can attest to how the beauty of Plitvice covered with snow and ice inspires a tranquil feeling of freedom.

One of the great things about Plitvice Lakes is that the park is accessible from nearby Karlovac or from Zagreb. This close proximity coupled with the frequent and inexpensive bus lines make the park an easy getaway for

*Overhead view
of Plitvice*

Plitvice in wintertime

the day. Several buses leave in the early morning from Zagreb and also pass through and stop at Karlovac, getting you to Plitvice before lunchtime. There are several food options at the park, both on and off the premises, including large hotel complexes and buffet eateries. Many Croats take the opportunity to stop at Plitvice on the way to the coast to eat a tasty lunch or to rest for the night. Inside the park there are several opportunities for eating, drinking, and relaxation. The entrance fee includes a ferry boat ride across one of the park's largest lakes as well as unlimited rides on the park buses; both the ferry boat and the buses stop at locales with full tourist amenities, including outdoor benches, modern restroom facilities, large or small eateries, and souvenir shops.

Another great thing about Plitvice is that the park is kept immaculate and in harmony with nature. The walking paths twist downward for several miles in and around the lakes, as if in a maze, providing both up-close views of the waterfalls and plant life and faraway panoramic views of the lakes surrounded by the mountains. The series of lakes, with a continuous drop in elevation down to almost three hundred feet, are divided into the upper and the lower lakes. Waterfalls, both big and small, connect each of

Waterfalls and lake in Plitvice Lakes National Park

the lakes, forming one large body of water spread out across hundreds of acres of land.

The park could take days to fully explore, and such an extended period of time would not be wasted; it is possible, however, to see a great deal in as little as six hours, walking from the main entrance and then taking the ferry and the bus to help cover the distance to the upper lakes.

If you decide to remain based in Zagreb and take a trip to Plitvice for the day, here are a few important travel hints. Check with the information desk at the bus station in Zagreb to confirm the times of the buses both from Zagreb to Plitvice and vice-versa. You can buy your ticket to Plitvice, but most likely the bus will continue on to cities such as Knin or Split and will be labeled as such. The bus driver will announce the arrival to Plitvice and drop you off at the main entrance. Take note that across the street from this drop-off point is a small brown house—this is the bus stop for the return to Zagreb. To return to Zagreb, wait for the bus by this stop. While buses should stop as soon as they see a passenger waiting there, it might be a good idea to wave at the bus driver so he knows that you are waiting for a long-distance bus and not for a local city bus or taxi. You can buy the return ticket on the bus and then sit back and relax.

If you decide to spend more time in Plitvice, you can explore the beautiful surrounding countryside, along with the small towns in the area, which are quaint and offer a lot to see. Plenty of restaurants and accommodations exist here. Just look for signs saying **sobe**, **Zimmer**, or **rooms**—these could refer to a hotel or a private room in a house. In this area the food is typically hearty and favors meat dishes, so don't be surprised to see a lot of **odrezak** (*oo-dray-zack*), steak, *schnitzel*, and few, if any, vegetarian platters or light soups. There may even be a restaurant serving **srnetina** (*sir-neh-tee-nah*), "venison," or other wild game found in the area.

Check out the park's official Web site at: www.np-plitvicka-jezera.hr.

Krka

The next national park to visit is **Krka**, located in southern Croatia. Krka is home to a wonderful variety of flora (860 species and subspecies verified at the park) and fauna (18 varieties of fish) and has seven waterfalls dropping a total of almost 750 feet. One of the most interesting attractions at

Monastery at Krka

the park—besides the Roman ruins and numerous nature trails—is the **Franciscan monastery** located on a small island in the middle of the lake. Accessible during the peak tourist season, the monastery is a unique aspect to this park's rich heritage.

Kopački rit

Another park of interest on the mainland is **Kopački rit** (*co-patch-key writ*), located near the Serbo-Croatian border. This park is a biologist's dreamworld. As a floodplain for the mighty Danube River, this area of forests, swamps, rivers, and lakes offers the eco-tourist a wealth of possibilities. Aquatic animals, land-based animals, and migratory birds all make this flood basin home for at least part of the year. The diversity at any given time is tremendous and the constant changes—thanks to varying levels of flood waters—offer the nature lover a truly unique experience. Check out the very thorough Web site for this park at www.kopacki-rit.com.

Kornati National Park

The final national park of general interest to tourists is Kornati National Park, a series of eighty-nine islands in the Adriatic, which offers a lovely and rich landscape and is home to a spectacular submarine environment. The nearest cities on the mainland include Biograd and Zadar, where there are good ferry connections to Kornati. With a rich and amazingly diverse seabed, the park guarantees divers the time of their lives. Because of the fragility of this underwater world, the Croatian government enforces rigid protective measures for the park, and divers must contract with an authorized agency. The rules are strict, but these regulations help to preserve a truly wondrous ecosystem: night diving is not allowed, and it is forbidden to do anything to harm the park intentionally (such as leaving behind waste or harassing the sea creatures).

Above sea level, the tourist will find all necessary amenities. The landscapes are beautiful and reveal an astonishing diversity of plant and animal life. As with the diving, there are many regulations designed to prevent harm to the environment in the park, but these do not interfere at all with the quality of a visit. You can explore natural wonders such as the "crown"—a vertical rock formation jutting from the Adriatic—or you can wander through historic settlement communities complete with a Byzantine-era church.

THERMAL BATHS

A thermal bath generally refers to a warm body of water, which is believed to have special health-giving properties. Many wellness resorts advertise the presence of a thermal bath as part of their offerings, but be aware that a wellness resort will also provide a host of other wellness facilities, typically with a holistic approach to health.

Some information on **toplice** (*top-leet-sah*), spas, and thermal baths in Croatia can be found at www.toplice.com.

Links to Thermal Baths in Croatia

www.biokovka.hr
www.bizovacke-toplice.hr

www.bolnicastubicketoplice.com
www.daruvarske-toplice.hr
www.hotel.hr/kalos
www.hotel-croatia.hr
www.hupi.hr/talaso
www.istarske-toplice.hr
www.krapinske-toplice.htnet.hr
www.ljeciliste-topusko.com
www.naftalan.hr
www.solaris.hr
www.terme-tuhelj.hr
www.thalassotherapia-opatija.hr
www.toplicesvetimartin.hr
www.varazdinske-toplice.hr

Scuba Diving

If you are a fan of diving, Croatia is the place to be during the summer due to the lengthy coastline offering seemingly endless possibilities for exploration in the underwater world. Check out some of the Web sites to see which ones have the most attractive diving opportunities (given your level of experience, cost, and the diving environment).

Useful Web Sites

www.adriatica.net/croatia/feature/ronjenje_en.htm
www.big-blue-sport.hr
www.bougainville.nl
www.diving.hr
www.dolphin-divers.de
www.manta-diving.com
www.marinesport.hr
www.mihuric.hr
www.mirkodivingcenter.com
www.nadji-laguna.com

www.nenodiving.com
www.tauchinjelsa.de
www.trogirdivingcenter.de
www.wakeboarder.hr

Hiking and Climbing

Remember that Croatia was at war until 1995. Although mine-clearing projects have accomplished a great deal toward making Croatia more secure, do take into account that there are still some regions that are not totally safe. For further information, contact the Croatian Demining Center, "**Hrvatski centar za razminiranje**," Ante Kovačića 10, 44 000 Sisak +385 44 554 151, hcr@hcr.hr, www.hcr.hr.

If the area is approved and clear of any mines, hiking is a real treat because the natural beauty of the forests is amazing, and the mountains and countryside will surprise you with spectacular panoramas, a lively natural environment, and fresh air.

Sailing

Croatia can rightly be called a haven for boaters because of the richness of the coastline, its historic cities on the shores, and the countless islands that keep beckoning to the traveler. The Croats recognize that boating offers many advantages for tourists, and that more tourists mean a better economy; with that in mind, the authorities are constantly updating and expanding boating services. Croats historically looked outward to the sea for a livelihood, and so it is not surprising that the tourist can take advantage of a complex sea-based economy. It is easy to rent a boat in Croatia after taking care of the few bureaucratic procedures (such as showing a recreational craft license, obtaining a radio certificate, and providing a crew list). The process is not difficult, and the appropriate authorities exist at all the harbors throughout Croatia, from the biggest cities such as Split to the sleepy ports such as Mali Lošinj.

From the comfort of your boat, you can sail up and down the coast at your own pace while checking out all of the hot spots. You can explore Dubrovnik

Sailing on the Adriatic

and the nearby islands, make the short voyage to beautiful Mljet and Korčula islands, and leisurely sail up to Split to enjoy music events, parades, and all the special events of a large city. A nautical adventure would be incomplete without a short visit to the "old towns" such as Korčula along with time spent sailing around the island—maybe even including a short diving session in any one of a number of pristine lagoons.

Sailing also allows for exploration of the beautiful midsection of Croatia's coastal area, centered on the city of Zadar. From here you can travel north to the islands of Rab, Krk, and then on to Rijeka and the Istrian peninsula. The numerous small fishing villages in the northern coastal area are astounding in their natural and simple beauty. Taken in tandem with the bustling port of Rijeka, the luxurious tranquility of Pula, and Rovinj and the historic island town of Krk, these provide for a unique experience.

The opportunities for taking full advantage of a sailing trip are enormous—the open waters provide the flexibility to personally craft your vacation at a leisurely and unique pace. You don't need to worry about crowded buses, jammed highways, or hard-to-find hotel rooms. When you wish, you can retreat to your vessel and make the trip your very own.

For information on sailing, visit the Croatian National Tourist Board (www.croatia.hr/English) to get going on this sea-based adventure!

PART III

Eating Out

CHAPTER 10

INTRODUCTION TO CROATIAN CUISINE

On the following pages we would like to introduce you to the types of eating and drinking establishments that exist in Croatia—**restoran, gostionica, konoba, pizzerija, riblji restoran, menza** (or **ekspres restoran**), **fish buffet, slastičarnica, pekarna, kavana, kafić, bar, klub, pivnica**—and some methods for choosing good ones.

Croatia has a wide variety of places to eat, drink, and have fun. But be careful, because a long menu is not always proof of either good or satisfying dishes. While this is not as common along the coast or in other highly touristy places, long menus do not in fact always mean that everything is available; sometimes only a few of the dishes offered can in fact be ordered. Don't despair. The waiter will let you know what is not available, and you can also check by taking a quick look around. Is everyone else eating the same kind of pizza? If so, it may be safe to assume that pizza is all the chef is cooking that night.

The many restaurants in the city center or at the **riva**—the promenade along the water—are the kinds of places you are likely to visit during your vacation. Just as in the United States, such popular destinations may turn out to be dreaded "tourist traps" that offer expensive yet low-quality food. There will always be restaurateurs or barkeepers who are locked into the old-fashioned conviction that only the present matters, and that tourists are not repeat customers.

This is unfortunate anywhere you go, but fortunately, it is not very difficult to cope with this problem in Croatia. So do always keep your eyes open and try to understand the Croats. They know that they have a beautiful coastline, and they also spend their own holidays there. The authors can assure you that thanks to the abundance of local tourists, it will be easy to spot the tourist traps by simple observation. Try to keep your eye out for bars and restaurants where the majority of people are speaking Croatian, and avoid the places catering only to foreigners. While this is a general rule, we do not wish to blacklist establishments that cater to a foreign audience. Some of the more upscale restaurants and bars will be full of foreigners because the prices are too high for locals. Another thing to keep in mind is that because of the sheer number of foreign tourists, it may be difficult to locate the places

Example of an outdoor menu

where Croats go. Going for what looks good is better advice than any five-star window sign or suggestion in a travel brochure. After only a few days in Croatia, you will be able to recognize Croatian, and to see the difference between really good establishments and tourist traps. Another tip: take a moment to observe the parking lot, if the restaurant has one. Are there any Croatian license plates? If not, it is probably not a good restaurant or not Croatian. Overall, Croats are friendly to tourists, and we recommend that whenever you get the chance to talk to locals or people who spend every summer in the same coastal village (and there are thousands who do this) feel free to ask them about places that they recommend. "**Znate li gdje ima dobar riblji restoran?**" (*znah-te lee gah-deyeah ee-mah dough-bar rib-lee-e res-tour-an*), "Do you know where there is a good fish restaurant?" or "**Možete mi nešto preporučiti?**" (*mo-zhe-tay me nesh-toe pray-poor-ooch-eatee*), "Can you recommend something?"

You may at first be happy to note the number of signs denoting the acceptance of credit cards. If you see a "Credit Cards Welcome" sticker at the entrance, however, be sure to ask the waiter in advance to confirm that. In Croatian, you would say "**Može se platiti karticom?**" (*mo-zhe se pla-tea-tea car-tea-som*), "Can I pay with a credit card?" For more on paying, see Chapter 17.

Table setting at an outside restaurant in Dubrovnik

Now, we invite you to get to know more about the different types of eating and drinking establishments in Croatia! **Dobar tek** (*dough-bar tech*): *Enjoy!*

RESTORAN / RESTAURANT

There are three main types of general restaurants (**restoran** [*res-tour-an*]): **gostionica, konoba,** and **pizzerija.** A **gostionica** (*gost-e-own-itsa*) is a typical Croatian restaurant that you will find everywhere. You can even smell it when traveling around the country! Believe it or not, many of these lie just a few feet away from the main roads. And your trip will be much more enjoyable if you are not in a hurry and do not travel on the major highways. The only conveniences on the highway are at typical rest stops, and here you will not find traditional roadside restaurants. The more traditional places to eat—places where you find **odojak** (*o-dough-yak*), "whole piglet," or **janjetina** (*yan-yey-tea-na*), "lamb grilling in large ovens or spit-roasted," are along smaller roads. Don't despair. Traveling by road in Croatia is easy and the road signs are frequent and clear. You won't get lost; instead you'll just find more gostionicas. Try to plan for a break of about two hours, because after a big portion of pork or lamb served with salad, french fries, and bread you might need a nap. So, take your time and enjoy!

Along the coast you will find what is called a **konoba** (*co-know-bah*). Konobas offer both Croatian and well-known international foods. You can dine on Croatian specialities and international favorites such as spaghetti, goulash, or a hamburger. The main difference between a konoba and a gostionica is that the konobas are found along the

Roadside roast—delicious!

coast and offer fish dishes. As a result, these are the most tourist-friendly eateries and are sure to offer something that you like.

Everywhere in Croatia you will find a **pizzerija** (*pizza-ria*) that offers inexpensive and fast meals. Depending on the restaurant, it may offer only different varieties of pizza or might include a range of Italian dishes such as spaghetti.

RIBLJI RESTORAN / FISH RESTAURANT

Fish restaurants (**riblji restoran** [*rib-lia-e res-tour-an*]) offer a wide selection of fresh, fine-quality fish. If you get up early, you can go to the harbor and watch the sailors coming in with their bounty and the cooks buying the fresh fish. At the **Obalno šetalište Franje Josipa** (*o-bahl-know set-al-ish-tah Frahn-ye yo-sip-ah*), a walkway on the Opatijan Riviera, you can sit a few feet away from the sea. Imagine sitting under an umbrella on the waterfront smelling the sea, enjoying the wide-open scene over the bay, and enjoying grilled fish while sipping from a nice glass of wine …

Typically, if a restaurant serves only fish specialties, the menu or signs will give a good indication of this; and these signs are generally located outside the restaurant to inform potential patrons of the dishes available.

Ribice / Fish from a Mobile Vendor

Another place where you can eat fish, though a special kind of fish, is from various street vendors. Resembling American-style hotdog stands, these mobile units bring the fish to you. They are generally located either in busy parks or at the beach and serve only small fish called **ribice** (*rib-eat-zay*). The two main types served include **srdele** (*ser-dell-lay*), "anchovies," and **gavuni** (*gah-voon-ee*), which are small fish in snack form. These fish are all fried, served whole, and are perfectly safe. Ask for bread ("**Kruh, molim!**" [*crew moe-lihm*]) and something refreshing to drink.

Slastičarnica / Ice Cream Shop

Although a lot of restaurants offer at least one or two desserts including **sladoled** (*slad-o-led*), better known as ice cream, we suggest you enjoy your dessert in a **slastičarnica** (*slas-ti-char-nitsa*), "ice cream shop." Some slastičarnicas also offer a wide selection of delicious cakes, pies, and tortes in addition to ice cream. Generally speaking, even in the most luxurious slastičarnicas the prices are low and the desserts are fantastic. If you are having a hard time choosing from the many varieties of dessert cakes, do not be shy; instead, approach the counter filled with desserts, known as a **vitrina** (*vee-tree-nah*), and point out your desired dessert to the waiter:

Ice cream creation!

This one please!	**Ovo, molim!** (*ovo moe-lihm*)
To the right!	**Desno!** (*des-know*)
To the left!	**Lijevo!** (*lee-ahvo*)
Down!	**Dolje!** (*doe-lee-ah*)
Up!	**Gore!** (*gore*)
That is right!	**Točno!** (*toch-know*)

Pekarna / Bakery

The bakeries (**pekarna** [*pay-car-nah*]) are great inventions because they both offer well-known items such as **kruh** (*crew*), "freshly baked bread," **sendvič** (*send-veech*), "sandwiches," and pizza, as well as local favorites such as **štrudla** (*shtrew-d-lah*), "strudel," **krafna** (*kraff-nah*), "doughnut," or **kifla** (*keef-lah*), light and fluffy "crescent rolls." The baked goods are sold at a very fair price and many of the bakeries—at least in the cities—are open all night long. So after a romantic walk along the coast or following a great party in Zagreb, you will not have to go to bed hungry.

The authors of this book have both lived in Zagreb and believe that there is a lot you can live without, but not bakeries. The fresh pastries offer a late-night snack on the way home and are also a great way to enjoy breakfast. What better way to start off your day than to get a **čokoladni puž** (*choco-lad-knee puzsh*), a local speciality similar to a chocolate-filled doughnut, or a **slanac** (*slan-ats*), similar to an American carnival-style pretzel, and eat it in a nearby café along with coffee?

Kavana / Kafić / Café

It seems that for Croatian men the typical goals of building a house, planting a tree, and having a child no longer apply. Instead, they choose to open at least three cafés during their lifetime. Even a small café—**kafić** (*kah-feach*) or **kavana** (*ka-van-ah*)—boasts a menu that would make Starbucks jealous. You will never go thirsty in Croatia because there are literally thousands of cafés, and you can sit outside all year long, even in a chilly winter, because of outdoor heating and the wide availability of alcoholic beverages.

Café traffic

People in Croatia endlessly bicker about the **bura** (*boh-rah*), crisp northerly wind, or **jugo** (*you-gah*), warm southerly wind—the typical winds in Croatia. You can find refuge from these drafty winds in the countless cafés across the country. They will be filled with people chatting, doing business, or just relaxing—the perfect atmosphere that makes the cafés unbeatable. It is one of the easiest ways to get to meet people, so use these opportunities to ask, "**Odakle ste Vi?**" (*oh-dak-lea stay vee*), "Where are you from?" and follow up with, "**Ja sam iz Amerike / iz Bostona**" (*jah saam eeze Amer-ee-ka / Boston-a*), "I am from America / from Boston," or the like.

BAR

Because of the large number of cafés in Croatia there is actually no need for another type of watering hole. But there are American-style bars serving liquor—including favorites such as Jack Daniels—in larger hotels and in cities such as Zagreb. Because cafés have diverse menus that include coffee, tea, soda, juice, beer, and spirits, a typical American-style bar is harder to find, and most of those that do exist specialize in long drinks. As is the case everywhere, the bars may also be home to inebriated people singing or dancing either on their own initiative or as part of a karaoke special. There are also numerous so-called Irish pubs that offer Irish-style décor, Guinness, and a generally welcoming atmosphere. Some also offer dancing and karaoke on certain days along with organized Irish dancing lessons (check out www. irskistudio.com). You will recognize these establishments instantly by the prodigious use of green along with clovers, Irish flags, and peculiar names such as the "Rusty Nail."

KLUB / CLUB

There are only a few real clubs (**klub** [*kloob*]) similar to the American norm, and while these are mostly found in Zagreb, they are now springing up in more frequented tourist spots such as Dubrovnik and Split. They offer a variety of American pop music along with Croatian favorites, and on the weekends they can be quite busy. There is seldom a cover charge, but the drinks inside do cost more than in other bars or cafés. Expect both a busy dance floor and a posh crowd unless you find an alternative club with gothic-clad patrons. There is also an emerging gay scene in Croatia, and while it may be difficult to find an establishment catering to gay, lesbian, bisexual, or transsexual clientel, such bars and clubs do exist.

PIVNICAS / BEER GARDENS

There are only a few real **pivnicas** (*peave-nit-za*), "beer gardens," to be found in Croatia, but they are well worth the visit. Besides traditional Croatian food, they offer a variety of beer from their own brewery in half-liter (16-ounce) or one-liter (34-ounce) glasses. This beer is not for the faint at heart. Many offer a selection of home-brewed beer ranging from pilsner or wheat beers to dark, rye-colored beers. Do not be surprised to witness patriotic singing or intoxicated bouts of love song recitals at all times of the day. Dive into the feelings of the people—either young, desperate soldiers, or men in their sixties lost in a different world!

Foreign Cuisine and Fast Food

Owing to the more recent discovery of Croatia as an international tourist destination, the variety of international food remains limited. This, of course, excludes Italian restaurants, since those can be found everywhere and offer the typical staples of Italian cuisine. Because the Italian restaurants are so common, many people don't really consider them international but rather as domestic, **domaći** (*doe-ma-chee*). The quality is generally comparable to Italian restaurants anywhere else, but these can be a bit less expensive than the norm.

Only in Zagreb will you find a variety of dedicated international restaurants, but with more tourists, the cuisines available in other cities are becoming more diverse. As stated above, **konobas** along the coast will offer a smattering of international dishes such as Wienerschnitzel (**bečki odrezak** [*bech-key ode-ra-zack*] in Croatian) or steak known as **biftek** (*beef-tek*). Only Zagreb offers genuine Mexican, Chinese, and other national restaurants.

You can, of course, stop in one of the many McDonald's restaurants throughout Croatia (mainly in Zagreb, but ever expanding). The menu will be familiar, but there are a few items intended especially to cater to the Croatian audience. For something similar, but bigger and less expensive, try a **pljeskavica** (*plea-es-kah-veat-zah*), which is loaded with more condiments than an American hamburger. Unfortunately, there are only a few dedicated pljeskavica places to be found throughout Croatia. When you find one, order and enjoy! The major Croatian fast food chain for pljeskavica and other grilled specialities is called **Rubelj Grill** (www.rubelj-grill.hr). Check their Web site for locations and information. One of the options when ordering pljeskavica is to ask for a special bread, similar to Greek pita bread, called **lepinja** (*lep-een-ja*).

Menza / Cafeteria

When traveling on a budget there are still several options in Croatia. There are some cafeterias, **menza** (*men-za*)—mainly in larger cities such as Zagreb and Split—where a decent meal can be had for very little money. Unfortunately, most of these cafeterias are closed during the summer. If you are not traveling to Croatia during the high season (summer months) you can ask around near the student dormitories or university buildings. Be aware, however, that the prices listed in the cafeteria generally do not reflect the cash price. Croatian students use their ID, called the X-ica (*iks-eat-zah*), which works like a debit card. Sponsored by the state, the X-ica card gives students a 75 percent discount. You will need to multiply the posted price by four, but even then the food is very reasonable. This is a budget way of eating with budget expectations. The food is acceptable, but don't expect tuxedo-clad waiters; a single menza in Zagreb serves up to 10,000 students just at lunchtime each day!

VEGETARIAN CUISINE

Although Croatia is opening up more and more to the expectations of Western tourists, there exist few vegetarian-only restaurants and hardly any vegetarian dishes in general.

If you plan a longer stay and would like to prepare your own spaghetti, vegetarian lasagne, or stews, rent an apartment and get fresh vegetables and fruits from the market. Most common are tomato, paprika, cucumber, and onions, in addition to local fruits such as figs, plums, grapes, cherries, melons, etc. And once again, enjoy the advantage of the twenty-four-hour bakeries ...

If you do not want to go to the market and cook for yourself or have a romantic picnic at the beach, there are the following possibilities for dining out:

pizza	**pizza** (*pee-zah*)
salad	**salata** (*sah-latta*)
baked cheese	**pohani sir**
vegetarian plate	**vegetarijanska plata** (*vege-tahr-e-anska plah-tah*)
cheese plate	**sir plata** (*sear plah-tah*)
fried mushrooms	**šampinjoni na žaru** (*sham-pin-yoney nah zhar-oo*)
spaghetti	**špageti** (*shpa-getty*)
garnishes	**prilozi** (*pre-low-zee*)

(For more, take a look at Chapter 16.)

Of course, you can try to get the cook to offer a special vegetarian menu by asking "**Imate li nešto bez mesa?**" (*ee-ma-tay lee nesh-toe bez mesa*), "Do you have something without meat?" or "**Ja sam vegetarijanac(m) / vegetarijanka(f)**" (*ya sahm vege-tar-e-an-ats / vege-tar-ee-an-kah*), "I am vegetarian." Our vegetarian testers really enjoyed a combination of **blitva** (*bleet-vah*), "chard," normally served with potatoes, and **đuveč** (*jew-veche*), a blend of paprika and tomatoes often served with rice.

So take your time, relax, and enjoy your meal: "**Dobar tek!**" (*dough-bar tech*), "Bon appetite!" and "**Živjeli!**" (*zheave-yelli*), "Cheers!"

Jelovnik

Salate

Miješana salata	10
Tunjevina	10
Sezone salate	11
Zelena salata	11
Kupus	9
Krompir salata	13

Juhe

Riblja juha	12
Francuska juha	13

Meso

Miješano meso	85
Teletina	65
Janjetina	55
Pljeskavica	45
Biftek	70
Pariški odrezak	65

Ribe

Orada	45
Pastrmka	45
Lignje	65
Ribice	35

Prilozi

Kruh	4
Pomfrit	9
Ajvar	5
Senf	5
Kajmak	6
Slani krompir	9

Pivo	14
Mineralna voda	11
Orangina	16
Coca Cola	15
Fanta	15
Schwepps	15
Capuccino	7
Espresso	6
Bijelo vino	22
Crveno vino	23
Rakija	14
Sok	18

Restaurant *"Hippocrene"*
Vranac Street Number 12
10000 Zagreb

Menu

Salads

Mixed salad	10
Tuna salad	10
Seasonal salads	11
Green salad	11
Cabbage	9
Potato salad	13

Soups

Fish soup	12
French-style soup	13

Meat

Mixed meat	85
Beef	65
Lamb	55
Seasoned hamburger	45
Steak	70
Paris-style schnitzel	65

Fish

Gilthead Seabream	45
Trout	45
Squid	65
Small fish	35

Garnishings

Bread	4
French fries	9
Ajvar (vegetable-based sauce)	5
Mustard	5
Kajmak (dairy cream)	6
Salted potatoes	9

Beer	14
Mineral water	11
Orangina	16
Coca Cola	15
Fanta	5
Schwepps	15
Capuccino	7
Espresso	6
White wine	22
Red wine	23
Brandy	14
Juice	18

CHAPTER 11

GOING TO A RESTAURANT

Generally speaking, in smaller cities nobody will be there to guide you to your table; instead, just go in and sit down wherever you please. In touristy places—especially during the high season—the employees will try to entice you into the restaurant from the street by showing the menu and inviting you to dine. Don't be afraid to say no and keep walking. You can always return to a restaurant, but be sure not to miss out on a really good meal by entering the first place that tries to solicit your business.

Once inside, don't despair if the waiter takes his time waiting on you. Just sit down wherever you want and after a few moments call the waiter loudly:

Molim vas! (*mo-lym vas*)   Please!
Jelovnik! (*yell-oave-nick mo-lym*)   The menu!
Konobar! (*coe-no-bar*)   Waiter!

In areas that are popular with tourists you will have no problem finding menus translated into English. If you need to ask the waiter for one, you can try:

Imate li jelovnik na engleskom?
(*e-ma-tay lee yell-oave-nick nah eng-les-com*)
Do you have a menu in English?

Here are some other vocabulary terms for dining out:

napkin	**servijeta** (*ser-vee-yet-ah*)
fork	**vilica** (*vil-eatsa*)
plate	**tanjur** (*tan-your*)
cup/glass	**čaša** (*cha-shah*)

knife	**nož** (*knozh*)
spoon	**žlica** (*zha-leat-tsa*)
ashtray	**pepeljara** (*pepp-el-yarah*)
tablecloth	**stolnjak** (*stoal-knee-ak*)
saltshaker	**soljenka** (*soul-yen-kah*)
cruet for oil/vinegar	**bošica za ulje i ocat** (*bow-sheet-tsa zah oo-lay*)
basket of bread	**košar za kruh** (*coe-shar zah crew*)

For a bigger group of people and for upper-middle-class restaurants in Zagreb and other bigger cities, it may be useful to make a reservation, especially at dinnertime on a Friday or Saturday. At the coast, restaurants that offer food **ispod peke** (*iz-poad pay-kay*), "under the stove," actually ask you to make a reservation for a specific time, as the preparation takes five hours or more. This involves either seafood or meat mixed with spices, oil, and garnishings put into a pot, which is covered with embers. This slow process of cooking makes the meat or fish soft and tender and brings out a flavor you won't soon forget! If you are lucky enough to find a place that does this—enjoy!

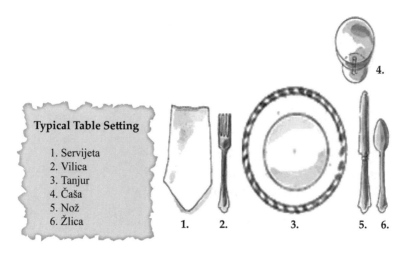

Typical Table Setting

1. Servijeta
2. Vilica
3. Tanjur
4. Čaša
5. Nož
6. Žlica

CHAPTER 12

ORDERING DRINKS

The various types of drinks, **pića** (*peach-ah*), will astound you during your visit to Croatia. From the many types of local beers to the different types of sodas and wines, you will never go thirsty! Cheers!

BEER

In most places, beer—**pivo** (*pea-voe*)—is cheaper than either soda or mineral water. This is in part because unlike Coca-Cola or Evian, the beer companies are domestic and beer is a popular beverage throughout the day. The domestic market for beer also must cater to a broad clientele whose wages have only recently risen toward Western standards (officially, the average Croat earns about US$600–800 per month). The beer is therefore fresh and inexpensive owing to the small size of the Croatian market. Expect to find several major varieties of beer, but by far the most famous is **Ožujsko.**

There are two main types of beer: **svijetlo** (*svee-ett-low*), "light," and **tamno** (*tam-know*), "dark." Some breweries also offer wheat beer, black beer, or red beer. Whenever you have a chance, try them. But the most famous beers that we can recommend are **Ožujsko** (*o-zhew-skoe*), **Karlovačko** (*car-low-vach-koe*), **Pan** (*pahn*), **Osiječko** (*o-see-ech-koe*), **Tomislavo** (*toe-me-slah-voe*) (dark), **Staro Češko** (*stah-row chesh-koe*), **Bavaria** (*bah-vah-rea*), and **Laško** (*lah-skoe*).

Ordering Beer

Ožujsko, please.	**Ožujsko, molim.** (*o-zhuj-sco mo-lym*)
From the tap.	**Točeno.** (*to-che-no*)

Half a liter.	**Od pola litre.** (*od po-lah li-tra*)
A small glass.	**Od nula tri.** (*od nuh-lah tree*)
Bottled.	**U boci.** (*oo botsy*)

WINE

Croatia is known for its fine wine, **vino** (*vee-know*), and the selection of both red, **crno** (*sir-know*), and white, **bijelo** (*bee-yellow*), wines is astounding. From large vineyards to family plots, the Croatian wine industry has a lot to offer.

If you like wine on a hot summer day try a **bevanda** (*ba-van-dah*), which is a mixture of red wine and water, or a **gemišt** (*gay-misht*), a mixture of white wine and sparkling water or club soda. Both drinks represent great ways to quench thirst following time in the sun.

We have provided you with a nice selection of excellent Croatian wines below, but the list is in no way complete owing to the continuing expansion of the already large wine industry. Don't hesitate to be adventurous, and just choose one in a market or a **vinoteka** (*vee–know–techa*), "wine store." The results should be promising. There are several levels of quality that correspond well to both price and taste. Cheaper wine should generally not be consumed without a mixer (water or cola). That said, Croatia is famous for some high-quality wines that we think are indeed hard to beat. The best is **čuveno** (*choo-veh-no*), and it will cost almost 100 kuna; the next grade is **vrhunsko** (*ver-hun-skoh*) and will cost a minimum of 50 kuna; the next level down is **kvalitetno** (*qual-e-tet-know*); the next two lowest are **stolno** (*stole-know*) and some without any marker.

Check the Web sites below for more information on Croatian wine:

http://korcula.net/vina
www.bastijana.hr
www.bluedanubewine.com
www.dalmacijavino.hr
www.istra.com/vino/eng
www.istra.com/zupan/eng/vinbuj.html
www.katunar.com
www.plancic.com

www.vinoteka.hr
www.zagrebacka-zupanija.hr/vina/eng

Primary Varieties of White Wine

Chardonnay (*char-doe-nay*)
Graševina (*grah-shea-vea-nah*)
Kujundžuša (*coo-whoon-jew-shah*)
Malvazija (*mal-vah-zee-yah*)
Muškat (*moosh-cat*)
Pinot (*pea-know*) / Pinot Sivi (*pea-know sea-vee*)
Pošip (*poe-sheep*)
Riesling (*reese-ling*)
Šipon (*sheep-on*)
Traminac (*trah-min-ats*)
Žlahtina (*zha-lah-tina*)
Žutica (*zhew-tea-tsa*)

Primary Varieties of Red Wine

Babić (*bah-bitch*)
Cabernet (*cah-burr-nay*)
Dingač (*din-gahch*)
Merlot (*murr-low*)
Opolo (*o-poe-low*)
Plavac (*plah-vats*)
Plavac mali (*plah-vats mah-lee*)
Postup (*poe-stoop*)
Refošk (*re-foeshk*)
Teran (*teh-ran*)

Dessert Wines

Maraschino (*maa-rah-schee-know*)
Pjenušci (*pea-yen-oosh-see*) (sparkling wine)
Prošek (*pro-shek*)

NON-ALCOHOLIC DRINKS

The proliferation of Coca-Cola over the last thirty years has rivalled that of nuclear weapons during the Cold War. Served and bottled almost everywhere, Coke continues to serve as the foremost American icon comparable only with Hollywood and blue jeans. Not surprisingly, Coke products are found in Croatia, but if you are a connoisseur, you will note a slightly different taste. This difference lies within the ingredients—rather than using high-fructose corn syrup as in the United States, Coke in Croatia is made with real sugar. Remember to brush after each meal to make your dentist happy!

Other common soft drinks include Schwepps Bitter Lemon, Fanta, and Orangina. You can also enjoy a nice lemonade, **limunada** (*lee-mun-ah-dah*), on a hot summer day.

If you ask for **voda** (*voe-dah*), "water," you will have several options; that is, either with or without gas. The carbonated mineral water is similar to seltzer, while noncarbonated water is just regular bottled water.

mineral water	**mineralna (voda)** (*min-er-alna vo-dah*)	
sparkling	**gazirana** (*ga-zeer-ana*)	
natural	**negazirana** (*ne-ga-zeer-ana*)	

How to Order Common Juices

Ja ću sok od . . .

orange	**naranče** (*na-ran-chey*)
bilberry	**borovnice** (*bor-ov-nitsay*)
apricot	**marelice** (*ma-rell-itsay*)
apple	**jabuke** (*ya-booh-kay*)
sweet cherry	**trešnje** (*tresh- knee-ay*)
sour cherry	**višnje** (*vish-knee-ay*)

If you thirst for coffee instead, you won't be disappointed. Skip ahead to Chapter 16, page 201.

CHAPTER 13

SOUPS AND APPETIZERS

Soups are referred to by two different names depending on the consistency of the dish. For example, soup could be called **juha** (*you-ha*) if it resembles a broth-like soup with chunks of vegetables, spices, and maybe some meat. **Čorba** (*chor-bah*), on the other hand, is a thicker soup with more substance. A type of popular čorba is **riblja čorba** (*ree-blea chor-bah*), "fish soup," which is a must for everybody spending a summer at the Adriatic Sea. Whichever soup you choose, you will be treating your taste buds well!

In addition to the soup, your server will most likely also bring you some bread to enjoy. Don't hesitate to dip your bread in the soup to soak up the flavor.

SOUPS

fish broth	**riblja juha** (*ree-blea you-ha*)
veal broth	**goveđa juha** (*go-vey-ja you-ha*)
cream soup	**krem juha od povrća** (*kre-em you-ha ode poe-vr-chah*)
French soup	**francuska juha** (*fran-souse-kah you-ha*)

APPETIZERS

Appetizers, **predjelo** (*pred-yellow*), are not all that common in Croatia, but you will find that the entrees are more than enough to fill you up. Some of the most frequent types of appetizers are cheese and prosciutto or special types of bread. Typically, Croats order a salad or soup instead of a traditional appetizer, but the most expensive restaurants will also have a wide variety of tasters.

cheese "trapist"	**sir "trapist"** (*sear trah-peast*)
prosciutto	**pršut** (*purr-shoot*)
beef tatar	**tartar biftek** (*tah-tahr beaf-tech*)
smoked salmon	**dimljeni losos** (*dim-lee-en-ee low-sose*)

Chapter 14

Entrées

Many options exist for creating a perfect Croatian entrée. From the wild game and more domestic meats to the exotic fish and family favorites, your dinnertime will always be satisfying! Whether you go exclusively to restaurants during your trip or cook for yourself at campsites or in apartments, you will not get tired of the possibilities from creative pizza specials, mixed meat grills, or fish on a platter. This chapter looks at the types of fish, meat, poultry, and other entrée options you'll find.

Fish and Seafood

An almost endless variety of fish, **riba** (*ree-bah*), and seafood, **morski plodovi** (*more-ski plode-ovee*), live in the lakes, rivers, and oceans of the world; however, in every country there are certain staples that are nearly always listed on the menus or that appear in the markets. Although the atmosphere close to the waterfront may be more attractive for first-time visitors to Croatia, hidden fish restaurants may offer the same and even better quality fish but with a quieter atmosphere and lower price. Just give it a try. Normally, you can begin with a fish soup or a salad and then dig into the main course featuring a big plate of mixed fish.

If the restaurant asks you to choose your fish by bringing it to your table on a small trolley, look at the shape, the size, and the smell of the fish to decide which one you would like; but normally every fish is fresh. The following list helps with choice, but do not miss out on the **škampi** (*shkahm-pea*), "shrimp," **punjene lignje** (*poon-yen-ay lig-knee-ay*), "stuffed squid," and **ribice** (*rib-ee-tse*), "small fish," which you will probably not find

189

Seafood platter

in every restaurant. Expect to wait a bit for your fish to cook; order a salad and bread along with some wine to prepare your palate.

Several styles of preparation are common, including these:

grilled

sa žara/na žaru (*sah zhar-oo/nah zhar-oo*)

boiled

kuhani/a/o (*koo-hon-ee/ah/o*)

roasted

pečeni/a/o (*pay-chen-ee/ah/o*)

smoked

dimljeni/a/o (*dim-lee-any/ana/ano*)

prepared in a pot in a stone oven, which is covered with hot ash

pod pekom (*poad pay-come*)

Common Fish and Seafood

(punjene) lignje (*poon-yen-ay lig-knee-ay*)

stuffed squid

bakalar (*bah-kah-lare*)

cod

brancin (*bran-tsin*)

sea perch

crni rižot (*sir-knee re-zhoat*)	cuttlefish risotto
dagnje (*daag-nay*)	mussels
gavuni (*gah-voo-knee*)	sand smelt (*small whitebait-like fish, usually fried*)
hobotnica (*ho-boat-nea-tsa*)	octopus
inćuni (*in-chew-knee*)	anchovy
jastog (*ya-stoge*)	lobster
jegulja (*yey-goo-lah*)	eel
konjski jezik (*con-ski yey-zick*)	halibut
kovač (*co-vach*)	Dory Fish
losos (*low-soas*)	salmon
miješana riba (*me-ay-shah-nah ree-bah*)	mixed fish
morski pas (*more-ski paas*)	shark
morski plodovi (*more-ski pload-ovee*)	seafood
orada (*or-ah-dah*)	gilthead seabeam
oslić (*oas-leach*)	European hake
ostrige (*oas-tree-gay*)	oyster
pastrmka (*pah-stirm-kah*)	trout
skuša (*skoo-sha*)	mackerel
rak/rakovi (*rack/rack-ovee*)	crab/crabs
ribice (*rib-ee-tse*)	small fish
riblja juha (*reeb-lee-ya you-ha*)	fish soup
rižot od plodova mora (*ree-zhoat ode ploh-doe-vah more-ah*)	seafood risotto
šaran (*sharr-on*)	carp
škampi (*skahm-pea*)	shrimp
školjke (*shkol-kay*)	shellfish
smuđ (*smoo-jah*)	perch
srdela (*sir-dell-ah*)	pilchard (*similar to a herring but smaller*)
tuna (*too-nah*)	tuna
zubatac (*zoo-bah-tats*)	snapper

Meat

While along the coast a wide variety of meat dishes may be a bit more difficult to find in restaurants, there are plenty of scrumptious options. But the best selection of meats is found in Zagreb and in the eastern parts of Croatia. Throughout the country, there are signs for pork or lamb on a spit at various roadside locales. If you can stop at one of these, by all means do so—you won't forget it!

Common Meats and Meat Dishes

(dimljena) vješalica pršut ([*dim-lee-en-ah*] *vea-shal-eatsa-purr-shoot*)	smoked prosciutto
bečki odrezak (*bech-key o-dray-zack*)	Wienerschnitzel
biftek (*beef-tech*)	steak
brizle (*breeze-lay*)	sweetbread (thymus)
burek (*boo-reck*)	meat- (or cheese- or spinach-) filled pastry suitable for lunch or an evening snack
ćevapi (*che-vah-pea*)	minced meat typically served with bread, onions, and ajvar
file medaljoni (*fea-lay meh-dahl-yo-knee*)	medallions
iznutrice (*ease-new-tree-tse*)	giblets
janjetina (*yan-yea-tean-ah*)	lamb
srnetina (*sir-neh-tee-nah*)	venison
govedina (*go-vay-deena*)	beef
juneći jezik (*yoon-ay-chee yea-zick*)	young beef tongue
junjetina (*yoon-yea-tean-ah*)	young beef
kobasica (*koe-bah-seat-tsa*)	sausage
jaretina (*ya-reh-tee-nah*)	goat
miješano meso (*me-ah-sha-know may-soe*)	mixed grill
mozak (*moe-zack*)	brains
musaka (*moo-sah-kah*)	moussaka
naravni odrezak (*nah-rav-knee o-dray-zack*)	nature schnitzel, breaded filet (topped with an egg)

odojak (*o-doe-yack*)	baby pork
pašticada (*pash-tea-sah-dah*)	beef stew with gnocchi
patka (*pat-kah*)	duck
pileći file (*pea-lech-ee fea-lay*)	chicken filet
piletina (*pea-lay-tean-ah*)	chicken
pljeskavica (*plea-yes-kah-vea-tsa*)	seasoned hamburger
punjene paprike (*poon-yen-ay pah-pre-kah*)	stuffed paprika
pureća prsa (*pure-ay-chah pur-sah*)	turkey breast
rebra (*re-brah*)	rib
roštilj (*roesh-till*)	grilled meat
sarma (*sar-mah*)	meat wrapped in grape leaves or cabbage
srnetina (*sirn-ay-tean-ah*)	venison
teleća jetra (*tell-ay-chah yea-trah*)	veal liver
teleći kotlet (*tell-ay-chee cut-let*)	veal cutlet
teletina (*tele-tean-ah*)	veal
tripice, fileci (*trip-ee-say, fea-lay-tse*)	tripe, filets
veprovina (*vay-proe-vean-ah*)	wild boar
zec (*zets*)	hare

Meat for Adventurous Travelers

bijeli bubrezi (*bee-yelli boo-bray-zee*)	testicles
mozak (*moe-zahk*)	brains
jetra (*yay-trah*)	liver

OTHER ENTRÉE OPTIONS

omlette (*om-let-tah*)	omelette
rižoto (*ree-zhow-toe*)	risotto
gnocchi (*know-key*)	gnocchi
tartuf (*tar-tuff*)	truffle
sir plata (*sear plah-tah*)	cheese plate
paški sir (*pash-key sear*)	famous cheese from the island of Pag

šampinjoni (*sham-pin-yee-onee*)	mushrooms
vegetarijanska plata (*vege-tar-een-ski plah-tah*)	vegetarian plate
zapečeni grah (*zah-pay-che-knee grah*)	baked beans
špageti (*shpa-get-tee*)	spaghetti
lazanje (*lah-zahn-yea*)	lasagne
palenta (*pah-len-tah*)	polenta

Please note that the designation for spaghetti with meat will most likely be listed as **Bolognese**, and meat lasagne might be listed as **lazanje s/sa mesom**. Cheese lasagne would be listed as **lazanje sa sirom**.

Pizza

One of the most popular entrees throughout the world remains pizza. While many Italians would cringe at the "pizza" prepared in many countries—including the United States—the basic concept is nonetheless prevalent almost everywhere. Croats make relatively good pizza, but it is not New York or Chicago style. Generally, Croatian pizza is not greasy and oftentimes the locals add ketchup or even mayonnaise. The toppings are otherwise consistent with what you can get in the United States.

sir (*sear*)	cheese
šunka (*shun-kah*)	ham
slanina (*slan-e-nah*)	bacon
špek (*shh-peck*)	white bacon
jaja (*jah-jah*)	egg
povrće (*poe-vrr-che*)	vegetables
ananas (*ah-nah-nas*)	pineapple
salame (*sah-lah-me*)	salami
masline (*maas-lean-ah*)	olives
luk (*louk*)	onion
češnjak (*chesh-knee-ak*)	garlic
gljive (*gah-lee-vay*)	mushrooms

CHAPTER 15

GARNISHES AND SALADS

One of the staples of Croatian cuisine is bread, and some kind of bread is served with almost any meal, even the most modest. Generally speaking, you will not find butter or margarine to spread on the slices of bread. Typically, oil and vinegar are used for dipping the bread, although it is very tasty eaten plain.

All of the basic garnishes, **prilozi** (*pre–low–zee*), are found throughout Croatia. Items such as **ajvar** (vegetable dip made from eggplant, peppers, and other vegetables) and **kajmak** (dairy-based spread made from cream and then fermented) are unique to southeastern Europe. The best **ajvar** (*aye-vahr*) and **kajmak** (*kay-mahk*) is homemade, but most restaurants will offer products found in stores. Ajvar and kajmak are typically used with **ćevapi** (*che-vahp-pea*), sausages served with bread, onions, and typically french fries, and **pljeskavica** (*plea-yes-kah-vea-tsa*), flavored minced-meat patties closest to an American hamburger, but can also be used on bread or with other meats.

GARNISHES

slani krumpir (*slah-nee croom-peer*)	salted potatoes
blitva (*bleat-vah*)	chard, Swiss chard
đuveč (*jew-vech*)	pepper and tomato mix often served with rice
kelj (*kail*)	kale
kruh (*crew*)	bread
pomfrit (*pome-frit*)	french fries
riža (*reezha*)	rice
šparoge (*shpar-roe-gay*)	asparagus

špinat (*shpin-aht*)	spinach
ajvar (*aye-vahr*)	vegetable dip
kajmak (*kai-mack*)	dairy-based spread
kečap (*catch-app*)	ketchup
papar (*pap-are*)	pepper
senf (*senf*)	mustard
sol (*soul*)	salt

SALAD

There are several options regarding salad, **salata** (*sa–lat–tah*), in Croatia, and each one of them will further whet your taste buds. Whether adorned with goat cheese or a selection of local vegetables, a salad in Croatia is, as a rule, great. There are some differences, however. The typical option in Croatia for salad dressing is not ranch, Thousand Island, or blue cheese; rather, you are provided with vinegar and oil along with salt and pepper. Only in the most tourist-oriented restaurants is there anything resembling American-style salad dressing, but even then the chances are slim.

Common Salads

miješana salata (*me-yah-shah-nah sah-laht-tah*)	mixed salad

Which may include:

grah (*grah*)	beans
krumpir (*croom-pier*)	potatoes
kukuruz (*koo-koo-rooz*)	corn
kupus (*koo-puss*)	cabbage
luk (*louk*)	onion
rajčica (*rye-che-tsa*)	tomatoes
paradajz (*para-di-ze*)	tomatoes
pomidor (*po-mee-door*)	tomatoes
sir (*sear*)	cheese

zelena salata (*zay-len-ah sah-laht-tah*)   lettuce

sezonske salate (*say-zone-skay sah-laht-tay*)   seasonal salads

pileća salata (*pee-lech-ah sah-laht-tah*)   chicken salad

tunjevina (*toon-yeah-vee-nah*)   tuna salad

grah salata (*grah sah-laht-tah*)   bean salad

Chapter 16

After-Dinner Options

As you can see from the short list below, plenty of dessert options exist but are not always available at any particular restaurant. Many Croats choose to indulge in **kava** (*kah-vah*), "coffee," **čaj** (*chai*), "tea," **pušenje** (*poo-shane-nyeh*), "smoking," or drink from a selection of spirits such as **rakija** (*rack-ee-yah*), "brandy." If a typical sweet is your cup of tea, the abundance of ice cream parlors and bakeries open late into the night will assure that you can always find a way to satisfy your desire for fresh, delicious, sugary treats. Your sweet tooth will thank you!

Desserts

(domaći) kolač (*doe-mah-chee co-lahch*)	cake
desertna kifla (*day-zert-nah keaf-lah*)	sweet croissant
gibanica (*jee-bin-eat-tsa*)	strudel with poppy seed, cheese, walnuts, and apples
kesten rolada (*kess-ten row-lah-dah*)	chestnut roll
krafne (*krahf-knee*)	kind of donut
kremšnita (*krem-shnit-tah*)	cream cake
čokoladna kremšnita (*cho-co-lahd-knee krem-shnit-tah*)	chocolate cream cake
zagrebačka kremšnita (*zah-grey-bach-kah krem-shnit-tah*)	Zagreb cream cake

palačinke (*pah-lah-chin-kah*)	crepe
pita od jabuke (*pea-tah ode ya-boo-kah*)	apple crisp
od marelice (*ode mah-rell-eat-tsa*)	apricot crisp
od maka (*ode mah-kah*)	poppyseed crisp
od šljiva (*ode shlea-vah*)	plum crisp
sladoled (*slah-doe-lead*)	ice cream
štrudla od sira (*shtrood-lah ode sear-ah*)	cheese strudle
od jabuka (*ode ya-boo-kah*)	apple strudel
od višnja (*ode veash-nyah*)	cherry strudel
štrukli (*shtrook-lee*)	cheese strudel
tiramisu (*tear-ah-me-sue*)	tiramisu
torta (*tore-tah*)	cake
čokoladna torta (*cho-co-lahd-nah tore-tah*)	chocolate cake
Esterhazy torta (*ess-tear-haa-zee tore-tah*)	Esterhazy cake (*Hungarian speciality*)
orah torta (*o-rah tore-tah*)	walnut cake
punč kocka (*poonch coats-kah*)	sweet dessert cake, typically filled with rum
Sacher torta (*sa-kerr tore-tah*)	Sacher tort (*Viennese speciality*)
Varaždinska torta (*vah-razh-din-skah tore-tah*)	cake from the city of Varaždin
voćna kocka (*voach-nah coats-kah*)	fruit cube
voćna salata (*voach-nah sah-lah-tah*)	fruit salad
voćni desert (*voach-knee day-zert*)	fruit dessert

After-Dinner Drinks

In addition to eating, drinking continues to be a popular after-dinner ritual. You can choose from a wide selection of good coffee or treat yourself to an alcoholic drink. While the list of wines or beers will remain essentially constant across Croatia, you will encounter different types of brandy in different cities and regions. Generally made from either plums or grapes, the brandies can be flavored with various spices or herbs or processed in ways that make them unique.

Hard Alcohol and After-Dinner Drinks

Loza (Lozovača) (*low-sah* [*low-so-vach-kah*])	grappa
Marelica (*mah-rel-eat-tsa*)	apricot brandy
Medovica (*me-doe-veat-tsa*)	honey brandy
Orahovac (*o-rah-o-vats*)	walnut brandy
Pelinkovac (*pell-in-coe-vats*)	herbal liqueur
Šljivovica (*sha-lee-vo-veat-tsa*)	plum brandy
Smokovača (*smoe-coe-vah-chah*)	fig brandy
Travarica (*trah-vahr-eat-tsa*)	herbal brandy
vinjak (*vean-yak*)	denotes some form of Croatian-made cognac

Coffee

capuccino (*cap-oo-chino*)	capuccino
espresso (*es-press-o*)	espresso
kava (*kah-vah*)	coffee
kava sa mlijekom (*kah-vah me-lee-ek-ome*)	coffee with milk
macchiato (*mah-key-ato*)	macchiato
produžena kava (*pro-doo-zhe-nah*)	two parts water and one part coffee

Tea

čaj (*chai*)	tea
čaj od šipka (*chai ode sheep-kah*)	rose hip tea
čaj sa limunom (*chai sah lee-moon-om*)	tea with lemon
čaj sa medom (*chai sah mea-dom*)	tea with honey

čaj sa šećerom (*chai sah she-cher-om*)	tea with sugar
crni čaj (*sir-knee chai*)	black tea
ledeni čaj (*lead-en-knee chai*)	iced tea
voćni čaj (*voch-knee chai*)	fruit tea
zeleni čaj (*zell-en-ee chai*)	green tea

In Croatia, you will encounter many smokers and encounter a culture that takes the production and enjoyment of spirits seriously. The preferred cigarette brands are Walter Wolf and Ronhill, with Marlboro Lights also popular but expensive. Strong cigarettes are generally avoided by Croats, as most prefer lights, ultra lights, and even super lights. After finishing a good meal, many people smoke several cigarettes while drinking a digestive such as plum brandy.

Živjeli! (*zheave-yell-ee*)	Cheers!

Chapter 17

Paying at Restaurants and Other Venues

When you finish your meal, sit back, relax, and enjoy yourself. As you have noticed by this point, service is rather slow by American standards, so the chances of the waiter coming by to ask you how you are doing or if you want anything else are slim. The one thing that the waiter will attend to is a dirty ashtray, but sometimes even this goes unnoticed. So after finishing your food and your beverages, you are ready to go. How to pay for the meal? What are the norms regarding gratuity?

Credit Cards

As stated earlier in the book, credit cards are becoming more common, and all major varieties are accepted throughout Croatia. American Express is as widespread as Visa and Mastercard. You will also see signs advertising Maestro, which is the debit version of Mastercard in Europe. If you don't see Mastercard but only Maestro, ask and chances are that your card will work. Know the regulations binding your credit cards before taking them abroad. Check the policy regarding the exchange rate; for example, does your card charge a fee for a transaction in a foreign currency? Make a copy of the front and the back of

Restoran "Hippocrene"
U. Vranaca 12, ZAGREB

Blagajna br: 012

---10.12.2006---18:08:52--BL1------

Račun br: 2543

Capuccino			
	1x	8	=8
Coca Cola			
	2x	12	=24
Pomfrit			
	1x	10	=10
Ukupno:			42,00

| PDV F 22,00% Osnovica: | 32,76 |
| Iznos: | 9,24 |

Gotovina
HVALA PUNO!

the cards that you take, and keep them in a separate place in case the cards are lost or stolen. That way, you have the critical phone numbers and can deal with an emergency quickly.

Having your credit cards abroad also allows you to access cash from banks if something happens to your ATM card. Any major bank in Croatia will be able to draw funds in any currency (dollars, kunas, or euros, for example) from your credit card.

Thus, if you want to use your credit card at the restaurant, it works in the same way as in the United States; but unlike in the United States, the receipt that you sign is final. There is no opportunity to add a gratuity to the bill once the waiter brings you the receipt. If the bill was for 75 kuna, you will sign the slip for 75 kuna and there is no place to add a 7 kuna tip. You must leave the gratuity in cash or tell the waiter beforehand to add a gratuity to the bill before processing the card.

Tipping

This brings us to the question of tipping. Do you always leave a tip? Tipping in Croatia, as in many other European countries, is voluntary and without set rules. Generally speaking, people leave a small tip if the service was good, but there is no set percentage that the waiter expects. This is also true for other services such as haircuts or taxis. If you want to you can give a few kuna to show appreciation, but in no way is this mandatory.

That said, the advanced tourist trade along the coast has made the trend of tipping more widely known among tourist industry workers there. In a small city like Osijek, in the Croatian hinterland, a tip would be unexpected and possibly even perplexing. But in a city such as Dubrovnik, on the coast, the waiter may think that if he serves an American, he will receive a tip no matter how good his service is. In the end, we advise you to use your judgment and tip accordingly. Do not feel obliged, and by all means do not feel that if you leave a tip, it must correspond to 15 or 20 percent of the bill. Five percent is sometimes more than enough.

TRAVELER'S CHECKS

Traveler's checks are not widely known in Croatia and the general rule is that businesses such as hotels or restaurants will charge a fee to accept your traveler's check if they accept it at all. To the best of the authors' knowledge, obtaining traveler's checks in Croatian kuna is not possible, so they must be used in the same way as dollars or euros. The benefit of traveler's checks is that if they are lost, you can contact the issuing authority (e.g., American Express) and they will cancel those checks and reissue you new ones with little hassle. At the same time, you can visit American Express offices (check their Web site at www.americanexpress.com for locations in Croatia) and exchange traveler's checks for cash in the local currency as more money is needed. The traveler's checks would not be accepted at any private money exchange office.

DEBIT CARDS AND ATMS

Here as with credit cards, check with your bank regarding its specific regulations, but generally speaking, a bank card can be used during a trip to Croatia. The fees for withdrawing cash may be high, but it is convenient to have the possibility of using the card. Most of the banks in Croatia are owned by international banks and therefore their machines have instructions in English and will recognize your card. The only real limitations on the card are those governed by your bank at home; for example, how much can be withdrawn each day. As for the credit cards, make sure you have the card number and the telephone number (if provided) in case of loss or theft.

As in the United States, your bank card should also work in restaurants and hotels with the amount being debited directly from your account.

KING CASH

As in most economies, the rule is that cash reigns supreme. Croatia is no exception. Soon after Croatia declared independence in 1991, it adopted a new currency called the **kuna** (*koo-nah*). The kuna is named after the ancient method of payment—that is, you would pay with marten pelts, or kunas. The notes are issued in denominations of 5, 10, 20, 50, 100, 500, and 1,000, while small change is 1, 2, 5, 10, 20, and 50 **lipa** (*lee-pah*), from the ancient form of payment using the bark of a linden tree.

If you pay with cash and the amount is, let's say, 7.92 kuna, and you pay out 8 kunas, you will not receive any change. In general, the very small change (less than 10 but sometimes up to 50 lipa) is not dispensed to close a transaction. On the flip side, if the bill is 8.08 kuna and you give the clerk only 8 kunas, you have satisfied your obligation. In the end, while this system seems ridiculous, any differences generally even out to everyone's satisfaction.

Chapter 18

Shopping at the Market, along with a Few of Our Favorite Recipes

If you are looking for a market you can ask: "**Gdje je tržnica?**" (*gah-dee-yay yea trzh-nea-tsa*), "Where is the market?"

Markets always have a special attraction, perhaps because of the crowd of people, or because of all the different sights and smells, or the sheer variety of things to buy. Sometimes it's hard to leave a market such as the big **Dolac** (*doe-lats*), the market on the uppermost side of Zagreb's main square. Once there, the traveler is hard put to stop trying the various types of homemade cheese, jams, and fruit snacks. The fresh fruits and vegetables are well-known for their taste, so get there early while there are still plenty of figs or cherries.

Shopping

When it comes to weights and measures, the issues get complicated and confusing. What constitutes a dash of salt or a jigger of rum? Well, there are excellent online tools that help to convert almost any size or measurement. For everyday use, shopping, and preparing some common recipes, we have provided a quick reference.

1 liter = 33.8 fluid ounces	1 ounce = 28 grams
1 fluid ounce = .029 liters	1 gallon = 3.78 liters
1 kilogram = 2.2 pounds	1 liter = .264 gallons
1 pound = .45 kilograms	1 quart = .94 liters
1 gram = .035 ounces	1 liter = 1.05 quarts

The logic of the metric system means that once you know the measurement in one unit, you can easily determine all other measurement values. For example, 1 kilogram of meat = 100 dekagrams = 1,000 grams.

How much does it cost?	**Koliko (to) košta?**	(*ko-lee-ko* [*toe*] *kosh-tah*)
How many/much is this?	**Koliko je to?**	(*ko-lee-ko yea toe*)
(*quantity*)		

When you're shopping, the first contact is an invitation and offer of assistance: "**Izvolite**" (*eaze-vol-e-tay*), "May I help you? / Please." Take a look and ask, "**Mogu li probati?**" (*moe-goo lee pro-bah-tea*), "May I try?" Normally the answer is "**Da, naravno.**" (*dah, nah-rav-know*), "Yes, of course."

When ordering, you can say, "**Pola kile smokava, molim**" (*poe-lah keal-ay smokah-vah, moe-lihm*), "Half a kilo of figs, please." Remember to use the genitive case when ordering food ... half a kilo "*of*" figs.

Often you may be asked, "**Još nešto?**" (*yoesh nesh-toe*), "Something else?" and your answer could be, "**Ne, hvala. To je sve**" (*nay, qua-lah. Toe yea svay*), "No, thanks. That's all." or "**Može još kila trešanja**" (*moe-zhe yoesh keal-ah treshah-knah*), "And a kilo of cherries."

The final part of the transaction involves determining the price: "**Dvadeset kuna**" (*dvah-day-set koo-nah*), "Twenty kunas." Now, here is the time to remember all of the numbers or simply hand over a large banknote to be sure not to reveal that you did not understand.

What kinds of things do you want to purchase at the market? Some of the best things to pick up are fresh fruits and vegetables, brought in from farms all across Croatia. Despite almost half a century of communist rule, which emphasized industry over agriculture, small family farms have survived and continue to prosper even to this day. The plums, apples, figs, peaches, and cherries are just the beginning. Fresh cabbage, tomatoes, lettuce, carrots, and grapes also beckon at the markets.

If you thought the French have a monopoly on good cheese, think again! Croatian farms are also well-known for processing cheese from their livestock, and you can try any one of a number of varieties. One of the favorites for Croats is goat cheese, which rivals that of Greece. Stroll the market and take a look at what the vendors have to offer.

RECIPES

After a successful trip to the market, it's probably time to prepare something "à la Croatia." Below are some of our favorite recipes: fish soup, pljeskavica, đuveč, and salad. These are all recipes that any traveler can prepare in a hotel with a kitchen or at a campsite. To find more recipes, check out some Croatian cookbooks, and for real Croatian ingredients at home, check out shops that ship to or within the United States such as Balkan Buy (www. balkanbuy.com).

Fish Soup / Riblja juha (*reeb-lee-ah you-hah*)

- 1.5 kg bijele ribe (*bee-elly rea-bah*) – white fish
- 200 g rajčice (*rye-chee-tsa*) – tomatoes
- a small amount of maslinovo ulje (*ool-yeah*) – olive oil
- 10 g češnjaka (*chess-knee-aka*) – garlic
- 1 limun (*lee-mun*) – lemon
- peršin (*pear-shin*) – parsley
- lovorov list (*loav-or-ov least*) – bay leaf
- sol, papar u zrnu (*soul, pap-are ooh tsir-new*) – salt, peppercorn
- 50 g riže (*rea-zheh*) – rice

Buy fresh fish, scale and clean, making sure to remove all the innards. Put the fish into a pot with water along with the tomatoes and spices listed above. Simmer for approximately 10 minutes, remove the fish, cut into small pieces, and put back into the pot (important: do not drain the pot during this process). Meanwhile, cook the rice in saltwater and when ready add that to the pot with the fish. Before serving, garnish with parsley and offer grated cheese on the side. Enjoy!

Pljeskavica (*plea-yes-kah-vea-tsa*) for Grilling

- 500 g teletine (goljenica *goal-yeah-nea-tsa*) or junjetine (bočnjak *boach-knee-ak*) – veal (shank) or young beef (flank), minced
- 100 g svinjetine (plećka *plech-kah*) – pork (blade), minced
- 100 g luka (*lou-kah*) – onion
- ulje (*ool-yeah*) – oil
- sol (*soul*) – salt
- papar (*pap-are*) – pepper

Prilog (*pre-loag*)—Garnishing

- 300 g luka (*lou-kah*) – onion
- lepinja ili kruh (*lep-eon-yah eel-ee crew*) – local flatbread or just white bread
- ajvar (*aye-var*) – local vegetable spread made primarily with eggplant and roasted peppers

Cut the meat into small pieces and mince it twice or just ask for ground meat at the market. Cut the onion into small cubes and add it, along with the other spices, to the minced meat. Mix and let stand 20–30 minutes. Now form thin, flat pieces, round in shape, approximately 6–8 inches in diameter, creating **pljeskavica**. Put oil on the grill or into a pan and fry or grill the pljeskavica up to 10 minutes, turning them twice. After frying or grilling the pljeskavica, soak up the remaining grease with the bread and add onions and ajvar.

Đuveč (*jew-več*)—Cooked Vegetables as a Garnish or for Vegetarians

- 500 g crvenog luka (*sir-ven-ah lou-kah*) – red onion
- 500 g rajčica (*rye-chee-tsa*) – tomatoes
- 500 g paprika (*pap-ree-kah*) – hot pepper
- juha ili voda (*you-ha eel-ee voe-dah*) – broth or water
- ulje (*ool-yeah*) – oil
- sol (*soul*) – salt
- papar (*pap-are*) – pepper
- Vegeta (*vey-gay-ta*) – mixture of Croatian spices
- ocat (*oats-at*) – vinegar
- riža (*rea-zha*) – rice

Slice the red onion and tomatoes into small pieces and start to fry the onions in a pan, add the paprika, and after 5 minutes add the broth and tomatoes to the frying mix. You can also use water and add salt and pepper or substitute **vegeta** (*vey-gay-ta*) instead and a bit of vinegar, so that it becomes sweet and sour. Cook until soft and add cooked rice.

Salata—Salad

- 300 g rajčica (*rye-chee-tsa*) – tomatoes
- 300 g krastavca (*kras-tave-tsa*) – cucumber
- 200 g ovčjeg sira (*oave-chee-egg sear-ah*) – goat cheese
- 100 g luka (*lou-kah*) – onion
- ulje (*ool-yeah*) – oil
- sol (*soul*) – salt
- ocat (*oats-at*) – vinegar

Cube the tomatoes, the cucumbers, and the goat cheese, add the sliced onions, sprinkle in a dash of salt, pour in a bit of oil and vinegar, and toss the mixture lightly. Voilà! You just made the most common salad on the Croatian coast.

PART IV

Language

Chapter 19

Useful Phrases

General

Yes.	**Da.** (*dah*)
No.	**Ne.** (*ney*)
Please.	**Molim.** (*moe-lym*)
Thank you.	**Hvala.** (*qua-lah*)
Hello.	**Bok.** (*boak*)
Good-bye.	**Doviđenja.** (*doy-vee-jen-ya*)
Do you speak English?	**Da li govorite engleski?** (*dah lee ga-vore-eat-tea eng-less-key*)
What's up?	**Kaj ima?** (*kai ee-mah*), for northwestern Croatia
What's up?	**Šta ima?** (*shtah ee-mah*), for the rest of Croatia
Do you know where I can find free rooms?	**Znate li gdje ima slobodnih soba?** (*znah-tea lee lee gah-day ee-mah slow-boad-neeh sow-bah*)
Do you have a phone card for the payphones?	**Da li imate telefonsku kartu za govornicu?** (*dah lee ee-mah-tay tele-phon-ska car-tah zah gah-vore-neat-sue*)
100 percent! Completely!	**Sto posto!** (*stough post-ough*)
Where are you from?	**Odakle ste Vi?** (*oh-dak-lea stay vee*)
I am from America / from Chicago.	**Ja sam iz Amerike / iz Čikaga.** (*jah saam eeze Amer-ee-ka / Chee-cah-gah*)

Travel Phrases

I am going to Split.	**Ja ću ići u Split.** (*ya chew ee-chee oo split*)
I am going to Opatija.	**Ja ću ići u Opatiju.** (*ya chew ee-chee oo o-paht-ee-you*)
One ticket for Opatija, please.	**Ja ću jednu kartu za Opatiju.** (*ya chew yed-knew car-too zah o-paht-ee-you*)
Two tickets for Dubrovnik, please.	**Ja ću dvije karte za Dubrovnik.** (*ya chew dvee-ay car-tay zah dew-brove-nick*)
When is the next bus for ...?	**Kada je sljedeći autobus za ...?** (*kah-dah yae sleigh-day-chee ow-toe-boos zah*)
When will we arrive at ...?	**Kada ćemo stići u ...?** (*kah-dah che-moe ste-che oo*)
Is this the bus to ...?	**Je li ovaj autobus za ...?** (*yea lee ove-eye ow-toe-boos zah*)
Wait a second!	**Čekajte malo!** (*che-kai-tay mah-low*)

Travel Vocabulary

airlines	**avionske linije** (*a-vee-on-ski lin-ee-ah*)
airport	**zračna luka** (*zrach-nah lou-kah*)
arrival(s)	**odlasak (odlasci)** (*ode-lah-sack* [*ode-lah-see*])
backpack	**ruksak** (*rook-sack*)
bag	**torba** (*tore-bah*)
baggage	**kofer** (*coo-fur*)
(main) bus station	**autobuni kolodvor** (*ow-toe-boose-knee co-load-vore*)
catamaran (does not carry cars)	**katamaran** (*cat-ah-mah-ran*)
choose the date	**odaberite datum** (*ode-ah-bear-eat-ay dah-tomb*)
(train) compartment	**kupe** (*coup-ah*)
departure	**polazište** (*poe-laze-eash-tay*)
departure(s)	**dolasak (dolasci)** (*doe-lah-sack* [*doe-lah-see*])
destination	**odredište** (*ode-red-eash-tay*)
ferry (that carries cars)	**trajekt** (*trah-yeckt*)
harbor	**luka** (*lou-kah*)

list, show, display	**prikaži** (*pre-kah-zhee*)
luggage	**prtljaga** (*purrt-lee-agah*)
pier	**pristanište** (*pris-tan-eash-tay*)
place/seat	**mjesto** (*me-ess-toe*)
platform	**peron** (*pay-roan*)
reservation	**rezervacija** (*rez-er-vat-sea-ah*)
ship (that does not carry cars)	**brod** (*brode*)
station	**postaja** (*poe-sty-ah*) / **stanica** (*stan-eatsa*)
ticket	**karta** (*car-tah*)
ticket office	**šalter** (*shal-ter*)
timetable	**vozni red** (*voze-knee red*)
train	**vlak** (*vlah-ck*)
train car	**vagon** (*vah-gun*)
(main) train station	**kolodvor** (*co-load-vore*)
waiting area	**čekaonica** (*check-ah-one-eat-tsa*)

SIGHTS

Where is the …?	**Gdje je …?** (*gah-dee-yay yea*)
art pavilion	**umjetnički paviljon** (*uhm-ee-et-neach-key pah-vill-ion*)
bloodbridge in Zagreb	**Krvavi most** (*curve-ah-vee moast*)
botanical garden	**botanički vrt** (*bow-tahn-each-key vert*)
bridge	**most** (*moast*)
castle	**trvđava** (*tver-jah-vah*)
church	**crkva** (*sirk-vah*)
lake	**jezero** (*yea-zer-oo*)
mosque	**džamija** (*jam-ee-yay*)
museum	**muzej** (*moo-zay*)
river	**rijeka** (*re-ache-ah*)
square	**trg** (*terg*)
stone gate (specifically in Zagreb)	**Kamenita vrata** (*kah-men-eat-sah vrah-tah*)
thermal baths, spa	**toplice** (*top-leet-sah*)
tower	**kula** (*coo-lah*)

Zagreb's inclined railway	**uspinjača** (*oos-pin-yah-cha*)
zoo	**zoološki vrt** (*zoo-o-losh-key vert*)
What can I visit?	**Što mogu pogledati?** (*shtoe moe-goo poe-glea-dah-tea*)

STORES & SHOPPING

What time do you open/close?	**Kakvo/koje je radno vrijeme?** (*Cac-voe/co-yea yea rahd-know vre-emmay*)
Where is the market?	**Gdje je tržnica?** (*gah-dee-yay yea trzh-nea-tsa*)
May I help you? / Please.	**Izvolite.** (*eaze-vol-e-tay*)
May I try?	**Mogu li probati?** (*moe-goo lee pro-bah-tea*)
Yes, of course.	**Da, naravno.** (*dah, nah-rav-know*)
Good, sweet!	**Dobro, slatko!** (*doe-bro slat-koe*)
Half a kilo, please.	**Molim Vas, pola kile.** (*moe-lim vas, poe-lah key-lah*)
Half a kilo of figs, please!	**Pola kile smokava, molim!** (*poe-lah keal-ay smokah-vah, moe-lihm*)
And a kilo of cherries.	**Može još kila trešanja.** (*moe-zhe yoesh keal-ah tresha-knah*)
This/that one.	**Ovaj/Taj.** (*o-vai/tai*)
Something else?	**Još nešto?** (*yoesh nesh-toe*)
No, thanks. That's all!	**Ne, hvala. To je sve!** (*nay, qua-lah. Toe yea svay*)
How much is it?	**Koliko košta?** (*coe-lee-coe kosh-tah*)
How many/much is this? (*quantity*)	**Koliko je to?** (*ko-lee-ko yea toe*)
Twenty kunas.	**Dvadeset kuna.** (*dvah-day-set koo-nah*)
Do you take credit cards?	**Mogu li platiti karticom?** (*moe-goo lee plah-tea-tea car-teat-some*)
Thank you.	**Hvala.** (*fah-lah*)
bookstore	**knjižara** (*kah-knee- zha-rah*)
pharmacy	**ljekarna** (*lee-ache-are-nah*)

PLACES TO EAT AND DRINK

bakery	**pekarna** (*pay-car-nah*)
bar	**bar** (*bar*)
microbrewery	**pivnica** (*peave-nit-za*)
café	**kavana** (*ka-van-ah*)
club	**klub** (*kloob*)
Croatian restaurant	**gostionica** (*gost-e-own-itsa*)
fish restaurant	**riblji restoran** (*rib-lia-e res-tour-an*)
pizzeria	**pizzerija** (*pizza-ria*)
restaurant	**restoran** (*res-tour-an*)
restaurant offering	**konoba** (*co-know-bah*)
Croatian and	
international food	
small cafés	**kafić** (*kah-feach*)

Do you know where
there is a good fish
restaurant?

Znate li gdje ima dobar riblji restoran?
(*znah-te lee gah-deyeah ee-mah dough-bar rib-lee-e res-tour-an*)

FAVORITE FOODS

bread	**kruh** (*crew*)
chocolate-filled doughnut	**čokoladni puž** (*choco-lad-knee puzsh*)
crescent rolls	**kifla** (*keef-lah*)
doughnut	**krafna** (*kraff-nah*)
ice cream	**sladoled** (*slad-o-led*)
pizza	**pizza** (*pee-zah*)
sandwich	**sendvič** (*send-veech*)
soft pretzel	**slanac** (*slan-ats*)
strudel	**štrudla** (*shtrew-d-lah*)

Choosing Food in a Case or Behind the Counter

This one please!	**Ovo, molim!** (*ovo moe-lihm*)
To the right!	**Desno!** (*des-know*)
To the left!	**Lijevo!** (*lee-ahvo*)
Up!	**Gore!** (*gore*)
Down!	**Dolje!** (*doe-lee-ah*)
That's it!	**Točno!** (*toch-know*)

In a Restaurant

A table for two, please.	**Za nas dvojica, molim Vas.** (*zah nahs dvoj-eatsa moe-lihm vahs*)
Can we sit there?	**Možemo li sjesti tamo?** (*moe-zhe-moe lee seys-tee tah-moe*)
Please!	**Molim vas!** (*mo-lym vas*)
Waiter!	**Konobar!** (*coe-no-bar*)
The menu!	**Jelovnik!** (*yell-oave-nick*)
Do you have a menu in English?	**Imate li jelovnik na engleskom?** (*e-ma-tay lee yell-oave-nick nah eng-les-com*)
Do you have something without meat?	**Imate li nešto bez mesa?** (*ee-ma-tay lee nesh-toe bez mesa*)
I am vegetarian.	**Ja sam vegetarijanac (m) / vegetari-janka (f).** (*ya sahm vege-tar-e-an-ats / vege-tar-ee-an-kah*)
Translation?	**Kruh, molim?** (*crew moe-lihm*)
Can you recommend something?	**Možete mi nešto preporučiti?** (*mo-zhe-tay me nesh-toe pray-poor-ooch-eatee*)
What is this?	**Što je ovo?** (*shtoe yea o-vow*)
I would like …	**Ja ću …** (*ya chew*)
Please.	**Molim.** (*moe-lihm*)
Thank you.	**Hvala.** (*fah-lah*)
Bon appetit!	**Dobar tek!** (*dough-bar tech*)

Cheers!	**Živjeli!** (*zheave-yelli*)
It's delicious.	**Odlično je.** (*ode-leach-know yea*)
Where is the bathroom?	**Gdje je WC?** (*gah-dee-yay yea vay-say*)
The bill, please.	**Račun, molim.** (*rah-choon moe-lihm*)
Do you take credit cards?	**Mogu li platiti karticom?** (*moe-goo lee plah-tea-tea car-teat-some*)

THE TABLE SETTING

ashtray	**pepeljara** (*pepp-el-yarah*)
basket of bread	**košar za kruh** (*coe-shar zah crew*)
cruet for oil and vinegar	**bošica za ulje** (*bow-sheet-tsa zah oo-lay*)
cup/glass	**čaša** (*cha-shah*)
fork	**vilica** (*vil-eatsa*)
knife	**nož** (*knozh*)
napkin	**servijeta** (*ser-vee-yet-ah*)
plate	**tanjur** (*tan-your*)
saltshaker	**soljenka** (*soul-yenka*)
spoon	**žlica** (*zha-leat-tsa*)
tablecloth	**stolnjak** (*stoal-knee-ak*)

For drinks, see page 183.

For soups and appetizers, see page 187.

For fish and seafood, see page 189.

For meats, see page 192.

For other entrees, see page 193.

For garnishes and salads, see page 195.

For desserts, see page 199.

For after-dinner drinks (including coffee), see page 200.

TIME

Seasons

spring	**proljeće** (*pro-lech-ay*)
summer	**ljeto** (*lee-ay-toe*)
fall	**jesen** (*yeah-sen*)
winter	**zima** (*zee-mah*)

Days

Sunday	**nedjelja** (*nay-dyeah-lee-yah*)
Monday	**ponedjeljak** (*poe-nay-dyeah-lee-ahk*)
Tuesday	**utorak** (*oo-tour-ahk*)
Wednesday	**srijeda** (*sree-ay-dah*)
Thursday	**četvrtak** (*chet-vir-tahk*)
Friday	**petak** (*pay-tahk*)
Saturday	**subota** (*sue-bow-tah*)
Week	**tjedan** (*tea-ay-dan*)

Months

January	**siječanj** (*see-ech-an-yeah*)
February	**veljača** (*vel-yach-ah*)
March	**ožujak** (*o-zhew-ahk*)
April	**travanj** (*tra-vahn*)
May	**svibanj** (*svee-bahn*)
June	**lipanj** (*lee-pahn*)
July	**srpanj** (*sir-pahn*)
August	**kolovoz** (*co-low-voze*)
September	**rujan** (*rue-yahn*)
October	**listopad** (*least-o-pahd*)
November	**studeni** (*stew-den-ee*)
December	**prosinac** (*pro-seen-ats*)

NUMBERS

1	jedan (*yea-daan*)	29	dvadeset devet (*dvah-day-set day-vet*)
2	dva (*dvah*)		
3	tri (*tree*)	30	trideset (*tree-day-set*)
4	četiri (*chet-rr-ee*)	31	trideset jedan (*tree-day-set yea-daan*)
5	pet (*peyt*)		
6	šest (*shay-est*)	32	trideset dva (*tree-day-set dvah*)
7	sedam (*say-dam*)		
8	osam (*oo-sam*)	33	trideset tri (*tree-day-set tree*)
9	devet (*day-vet*)	34	trideset četiri (*tree-day-set chet-rr-ee*)
10	deset (*day-set*)		
11	jedanaest (*yea-dan-es-et*)	35	trideset pet (*tree-day-set peyt*)
12	dvanaest (*dvah-nah-est*)	36	trideset šest (*tree-day-set shay-est*)
13	trinaest (*tree-nah-est*)		
14	četrnaest (*chet-rr-nah-est*)	37	trideset sedam (*tree-day-set say-dam*)
15	petnaest (*peyt-nah-est*)		
16	šesnaest (*shes-nah-est*)	38	trideset osam (*tree-day-set oo-sam*)
17	sedamnaest (*say-dam-nah-est*)		
18	osamnaest (*oo-sam-nah-est*)	39	trideset devet (*tree-day-set day-vet*)
19	devetnaest (*day-vet-nah-est*)		
20	dvadeset (*dvah-day-set*)	40	četrdeset (*chet-rr-day-set*)
21	dvadeset jedan (*dvah-day-set yea-daan*)	41	četrdeset jedan (*chet-rr-day-set yea-daan*)
22	dvadeset dva (*dvah-day-set dvah*)	50	pedeset (*pay-day-set*)
23	dvadeset tri (*dvah-day-set tree*)	51	pedeset jedan (*pay-day-set yea-daan*)
24	dvadeset četiri (*dvah-day-set chet-rr-ee*)	60	šezdeset (*shay-z-day-set*)
25	dvadeset pet (*dvah-day-set peyt*)	61	šezdeset jedan (*shay-z-day-set yea-daan*)
26	dvadeset šest (*dvah-day-set shay-est*)	70	sedamdeset (*say-dam-day-set*)
27	dvadeset sedam (*dvah-day-set say-dam*)	71	sedamdeset jedan (*say-dam-day-set yea-daan*)
28	dvadeset osam (*dvah-day-set oo-sam*)	80	osamdeset (*oo-sam day-set*)
		81	osamdeset jedan (*oo-sam day-set yea-dan*)
		90	devedeset (*day-vay-day-set*)

91   **devedeset jedan** (*day-vay-*
      day-set yea-dan)
100 **sto** (*stow*)
101 **sto jedan** (*stow yea-daan*)

111 **sto jedanaest** (*stow*
      yea-daan-ay-est)
120 **sto dvadeset** (*stow*
      dvah-day-set)

Appendix

Famous Croats

Sports Stars

Rudy Tomjanovic—NBA player and coach
Steve Stipanovich—former NBA player, No. 2 pick in 1983 NBA draft
Joe Sakic—NHL player (2001 Hart Memorial Trophy Winner)
Dražen Petrović—NBA Hall of Famer
Roger Maris—American baseball legend
Ivica Kostelić—alpine skiing slalom World Cup Champion (one Olympic silver medal)
Janica Kostelić—alpine skiing World Cup Champion in 2001, 2003, and 2006 (four Olympic golds, two silvers)

Important Croatian Politicians in Croatia and Abroad

Pope Sixtus V—pope from 1585–90
Dennis Kucinich—current U.S. representative from Ohio, former mayor of Cleveland (1970s)
Michael Bilandic—former Mayor of Chicago and former Illinois State Supreme Court chief justice (1970s)
Rose Perica Mofford—former governor of Arizona (late 1980s)
Rudy Perpich—former governor of Minnesota (1970s)
Michael Anthony Stepovich—former governor of Alaska (1950s)
Néstor Kirchner Ostoić—president of Argentina (since 2003)

Josip Broz Tito—head of Communist Party of Yugoslavia, guerilla leader
during World War II, and founder of Socialist Yugoslavia 1945–91
Franjo Tuđman—first president of modern Croatia, youngest Partisan gen-
eral under Tito
Stjepan Radić—head of Croatian Peasant Party following World War I
Josip Jelačić—Croatian duke and general who fought against rebellion in
Hungary (1848–49)

HISTORICAL CROATS

Nikola Šubić-Zrinski—military leader (1508–66)
King Tomislav—medieval king from 925–28 (duke of Dalmatia from
910–25)
Petar Krešimir IV of Croatia—medieval king of Croatia from 1059–74
Josip Juraj Strossmayer—cleric active during nineteenth century
Ljudevit Gaj—linguist who founded Illyrian movement in nineteenth
century
Faust Vrančić—(1551–1617) inventor of the parachute and first Croatian
lexicographer

ARTISTS AND PERFORMERS

Ivan Goran Kovačić—twentieth-century poet
Dubravka Ugrešić—modern writer and journalist
Slavenka Drakulić—modern writer and journalist
Severina Vučković—Croatian pop singer
Johnny Mercer—singer and song writer famous for songs such as
"Moon River"
John Malkovich—Hollywood actor, producer and director
Ivan Meštrović—(1883–1962) world-famous sculptor
Vanna White—Game show hostess from *Wheel of Fortune*
Goran Višnjić—from TV series *ER*

SELECTED BIBLIOGRAPHY

While tourism is a rather recent phenomenon, only coming to life in the second half of the twentieth century, the history of travel itself is both fascinating and rich. Some of the most famous travelogues appeared during Europe's intellectual and cultural awakening—the Enlightenment. While people searched for answers to life's questions, the journey oftentimes took them to many far-off lands. And naturally, traveling before the invention of modern machines meant weeks and sometimes months with little in the way of convenience. This was especially true of those adventurers who traveled east to the lands of the Russian, Austrian, and Ottoman empires.

Some of the most important names of the Enlightenment, such as Voltaire, looked eastward with great hopes. Later, other eminent figures, such as the brothers Grimm, the fabled Baron Munchhausen, and Jonathan Swift, all included in their works tales of mystery and darkness from eastern Europe.

To acquaint yourself with some of what eastern Europe has to offer, check out the following books at your local bookstore or online.

HISTORY AND CULTURE

Brown, J. F. *Surge to Freedom: The End of Communist Rule in Eastern Europe*, Durham: Duke University Press, 1991.

Drakulić, Slavenka. *How We Survived Communism and Even Laughed*, New York: W.W. Norton, 1992.

Goldstein, Ivo. *Croatia: A History*, trans. Nikolina Jovanovic, Montréal: McGill-Queen's University Press, 1999.

Jelavich, Barbara. *History of the Balkans* (Volume I and Volume II), Cambridge: Cambridge University Press, 1983.

Swain, Geoffrey, and Nigel Swain. *Eastern Europe since 1945*, New York: Palgrave Macmillan, 2003.

Tanner, Marcus. *Croatia: A Nation Forged in War*, New Haven, CT: Yale University Press, 2001.

Wolff, Larry. *Inventing Eastern Europe: The Map of Civilization on the Mind of the Enlightenment*, Stanford, CA: Stanford University Press, 1994.

LANGUAGE LEARNING & CULTURE: FROM HIPPOCRENE BOOKS

Pavičić, Liliana, and Gordana Pirker-Mosher, *The Best of Croatian Cooking*, New York: Hippocrene, 2007.

Šušnjar, Ante. *Croatian-English/English-Croatian Dictionary and Phrasebook*, New York: Hippocrene, 2005.

Vidan, Aida, and Robert Niebuhr, *Beginner's Croatian with 2 Audio CDs*. New York: Hippocrene, 2009.

Index

About the Authors

Robert Niebuhr is a historian and university instructor who has taught at Boston College, Simmons College, and Harvard University. In addition to modern European history and international relations, his academic interests include teaching South-Slavic culture and language at the university level. With several articles and book reviews, and a forthcoming book project on the history of Communist Yugoslavia, Niebuhr is also co-author with Aida Vidan of *Beginner's Croatian* from Hippocrene Books.

Bernd Scherak is a lawyer having specialized in eastern and southeastern Europe. A native of Austria, Scherak has made his career in law but has lived and traveled extensively in Croatia and Hungary, studying business, culture, and language. Involved in travel for purposes of cultural exchange, Scherak has made full use of his time abroad and tries to share the most important aspects of his experiences.

Also available from Hippocrene Books...

LANGUAGES TITLES

Croatian-English/English-Croatian Dictionary & Phrasebook
Ante Susnjar

This compact guide includes a two-way dictionary and a phrasebook with all the topics necessary for the traveler: food and drink, accommodations, customs, weather, health and more. Useful for both native English and Croat speakers, it provides the means for basic communication, as well as an introduction to Croatia's rich language and heritage.

272 pages • 4,500 entries • 4 x 7½ • 0-7818-0810-3 • $11.95pb

Hippocrene Children's Illustrated Croatian Dictionary
Hippocrene Books

The latest in the dictionary series that gives children a fun first taste of a foreign language.

- Designed to be the first foreign language dictionary for children ages 5-10
- 500 illustrated entries
- Allows a child to make the connection between a picture and the word
- Entries consist of the word in English, its Croatian equivalent, and easy-to-use phonetic pronunciation
- The vocabulary included covers the people, animals, colors, numbers, and objects that children encounter every day

94 pages • 500 entries • 8½ x 11 • 0-7818-1076-0 • $11.95pb

Beginner's Croatian with 2 Audio CDs
Aida Vidan & Robert Niebuhr

Beginner's Croatian with 2 Audio CDs is the only Croatian book-and-audio language instruction product on the market today. Includes:

- An introduction to Croatia
- Fifteen practical lessons with dialogues, vocabulary, and phrases
- Review exercises with answer key
- Croatian-English and English-Croatian glossaries

- Two audio CDs of dialogues and vocabulary with correct pronunciation by native Croatian speakers

352 pages • w/2 CDs • 5½ x 8½ • 0-7818-1232-1 • $29.95pb • available Summer 2009

Beginner's Serbian with 2 Audio CDs
Aida Vidan & Robert Niebuhr

The Republic of Serbia is located on the Balkan peninsula at the crossroads between Central, Southern, and Eastern Europe. The majority of its ten million inhabitants are Serbs and the official language is Serbian, written in both the Cyrillic and Latin alphabets. Serbia has a thriving tourist industry, driven by its scenic landscape, historical monuments, curative spas, hunting grounds, and fishing areas. Since 2001 Serbia has also attracted more business from around the world, with the U.S. as the largest source of direct foreign investment.

Ideal for tourists, business travelers, and students, *Beginner's Serbian* includes:

- A brief introduction to Serbian history and culture
- Fifteen practical lessons with dialogues, vocabulary, and expressions
- Instruction in the Cyrillic script
- Exercises with answer keys
- Serbian-English and English-Serbian glossaries
- Two audio CDs of dialogues and vocabulary spoken by native Serbian speakers

352 pages • w/2 CDs • 5½ x 8 ½ • 0-7818-1231-3 • $29.95pb • available Summer 2009

Beginner's Serbo-Croatian
Duska Radosavljevic Heaney

Serbo-Croatian, also called Serbo-Croat, was spoken in four of the six republics in the former Yugoslavia. It continues to be spoken in those geographical and political units, though there are slight variations in the vocabulary. *Beginner's Serbo-Croatian* is therefore an invaluable resource for students, businesspersons, and tourists traveling in Serbia and Montenegro, as well as Croatia and Bosnia.

Each lesson begins with a Serbo-Croatian conversation with side-by-side English translation, followed by an itemized vocabulary list, an explanation of expressions used, a section on grammar, and a listing of useful phrases.

A set of exercises designed to familiarize the reader with the grammar and vocabulary introduced conclude the lesson. Introductory chapters on the history and culture of the region complement this volume.

257 pages • 6½ x 9½ • 0-7818-0845-6 • $14.95pb

Serbo-Croatian–English/English–Serbo-Croatian Practical Dictionary
Nicholas Awde

- Over 24,000 entries
- Completely modern and up-to-date
- Concise, easy-to-use format
- Appendices of Serbo-Croatian and English irregular verbs
- Useful phrases

527 pages • 24,000 entries• 5½ x 8 • 0-7818-0445-0 • $16.95pb

Serbian-English/English-Serbian Concise Dictionary
Mladen Davidovic

- Over 7,500 total entries
- Phonetic pronunciation for each language
- Concise, easy-to-use format
- For travelers, businesspersons, and students of English or Serbian

394 pages • 7,500 entries • 5 x 7 • 0-7818-0556-2 • $14.95pb

Serbian-English/English-Serbian Dictionary and Phrasebook
Nicholas Awde & Duska Radosavljevic Heaney

Over the last several years, the Serbian language has been regaining its prominence in Serbia and Montenegro, as well as other parts of the former Yugoslavia. This guide, with its bilingual dictionary and comprehensive phrasebook, is an essential guide for students, travelers, and businesspeople.

- More than 6,500 total dictionary entries
- Comprehensive phrasebook
- Easy-to-use pronunciation guide
- Includes cultural information and a brief history of the language

239 pages • 6,500 entries • 4½ x 8 • 0-7818-1049-3 • $11.95pb

COOKBOOK

The Best of Croatian Cooking, Expanded Edition
Liliana Pavicic & Gordana Pirker-Mosher

Croatia, a beautiful and geographically diverse country on Europe's Balkan peninsula, offers sunny Adriatic coastline and breathtaking scenery, as well as a distinctive culinary tradition that combines central European, Mediterranean and Near Eastern influences. Meat lovers and vegetarians alike will find favorites among the over 200 easy-to-follow recipes featured here, from classic dishes like Strudel with Sautéed Cabbage and Potatoes with Swiss Chard to the famous Dalmatian specialty, Stewed Beef and Black Risotto, which is prepared with cuttlefish ink. Also included are over 50 dessert recipes for all variety of strudels, fine tortes, and cookies. The author's introduction to Croatia and its cuisine provides insight into the development of the culinary tradition through the centuries, as well as into the specialties of the various regions in Croatia. The addition of a chapter on Croatian wines completes the culinary tour offered though the pages of this book. Complete with b/w photographs. 10% of the proceeds from this book will be donated to War Child Canada for projects in support of children in the former Yugoslavia.

311 pages • 6 x 9½ • 978-0-7818-1203-0 • $16.95pb

TRAVEL GUIDES

Language and Travel Guide to Romania
Rosemary Rennon

With historical and cultural information, travel suggestions and a language guide, this book serves as an essential resource Romania. The guide features:

- 16 pages of color photos; information on transportation, hotels, dining and sightseeing
- Major tourist destinations Bucharest, Transylvania, Moldavia and many other significant but lesser-known cities and sites
- Cultural background detailing the lengthy and turbulent history and traditions of the Romanians
- A language guide to contemporary Romanian, complete with key Romanian phrases and words with a phonetic pronunciation guide

397 pages • 6 x 9 • 0-7818-1150-7 • $21.95pb

Language and Travel Guide to Ukraine
Linda Hodges & George Chumak

Originally published in 1994, this best-selling guide to scenic and culturally rich Ukraine has been completely revised and updated for this fourth edition. Detailed information regarding visas and customs, airlines, tours, hotels, shopping, sites of interest, insight into Ukrainian history, culture and local traditions, plus new color photos and maps make *Language and Travel Guide to Ukraine* a gold mine of information for travelers.

390 pages • 6½ x 9½ • 0-7818-1063-0 • $18.95pb

Language and Travel Guide to Sicily
Giovanna Bellia La Marca

Sicily, the pearl of the Mediterranean, attracts more than 1.5 million visitors each year. Known for its flavorful cuisine, pleasant climate, picturesque hill towns, rich ancient history, and flourishing arts scene, the island has plenty to offer all her guests. An excellent companion for travelers, this guide covers the region's major sites and cultural attractions and introduces the reader to the basics of the Sicilian language. Extensive travel sections cover major cities, events and festivals, hotels, restaurants, arts, and architecture. An introductory language guide includes grammar basics, useful vocabulary, and dialogues in both Sicilian and Italian. Two audio CDs provide clear pronunciation of the dialogues and phrases by native Sicilian and Italian speakers.

270 pages • 6½ x 9½ • 0-7818-1149-1 • $29.95pb

Prices subject to change without prior notice.
To purchase Hippocrene Books contact your local bookstore, call (718) 454-2366, or visit www.hippocrenebooks.com.